CW00521866

FIREPLACES

DESIGN AND CONSTRUCTION
OF DOMESTIC OPEN FIRES

B
Brailsford

Patrick Mitchell

FIREPLACES

DESIGN AND CONSTRUCTION
OF DOMESTIC OPEN FIRES

Brailsford

The moral right of Patrick Mitchell is asserted as the writer.
First published in Great Britain 2005 by Brailsford with WritersPrintShop
Reprinted with corrections October 2006

ISBN 1904623360

Designed by e-BookServices.com

**Dedicated
To Vic**

Preface

It is my hope that this book will equip the reader with a sufficient understanding of the principles of construction and operation of fireplaces for them to be able not only to build a standard design but also explore their own design ideas.

As important as understanding its operation is understanding the purpose for which a fireplace is built. This is usually for its appearance rather than heat output. Rarely in the western world would an open fire be built primarily as a heating appliance these days. Heating is a function best served by gas or oil fired boilers or stoves. This fact is not always acknowledged by people who see themselves as practical and unsentimental. Many times I have seen people who want a pleasing fire sold stoves on grounds of their superior efficiency only to be disappointed with the result because efficiency was not what they wanted.

Open fireplaces are the least efficient, most labour-intensive, and dirtiest of domestic heating appliances. These factors led to their widespread abandonment in much of the western world when alternatives became widely available in the middle of the 20th century. Their psychological appeal was largely forgotten or could not be accommodated in those days of relative austerity. As the century wore on and societies became more affluent, enjoyment became increasingly valued and fireplaces saw an increase in popularity. Sadly their fall from grace spanned more than a generation of architects, builders, and engineers. By the time fireplaces became popular again the skill base in their design and construction had been seriously eroded. As a consequence a substantial proportion of the fireplaces built the last 50 years are of a poor design and build quality. Happily this trend is now reversing.

There is one respect in which I depart from convention on fireplace design as presented in other books. That is with regard to the smoke shelf and smoke chamber. I consider them to be unnecessary and indeed slightly counter-productive. You will see my justification for this in later chapters and must judge the issue for yourself. I include details of smoke shelf design and construction notwithstanding.

Smoke control legislation has been a mixed blessing. There is no doubt that there has been an enormous improvement in the quality of the air we breathe in our cities since the first half of the 20th century. This is partly thanks to smoke control legislation that became possible because alternative heating systems were available. These were primarily gas and oil fired central heating systems. They are considerably more convenient, effective, and economical than open fires. They would have virtually universally taken over from open fires with or without smoke control legislation which effectively banned the use of solid fuel burning open fires in most urban environments in the UK. This was a significantly onerous imposition in a country with millions of installed open fireplaces.

Modern gas-fired technology has brought new possibilities for the enjoyment of flame in our urban environments. Living flame type gas fires are now so realistic that they frequently collect rubbish thrown onto them by people unaware that they are not real fires. The flexibility of gas has allowed fireplace manufacturers to use flame as an art form with stunning results and these advances have meant the welcome return of fireplaces to many of our homes.

TABLE OF CONTENTS

Chapter 1
Historical Background

Fires are among those aspects of life which, though essential, have not attracted much comment from historians. They have been used to heat buildings for countless centuries but the history of their development prior to modern times is poorly documented. This is particularly true of the technical development of fireplaces and their functioning. The history of fashions and styles in fireplace decoration is better documented* but less relevant to our present theme. What we know is derived from observations on old buildings and from occasional literary references which are rarely of a technical nature.

Improvements in fireplace design have been made empirically and have not depended on discoveries of general principles. Almost all of the developments that have occurred were introduced because they were found to work; the reasons why they worked were often not understood for centuries.

The recorded history of fireplace design in the western world begins with the Romans, partly because they were meticulous historians and partly because they were the first civilisation to expand into areas where effective heating was necessary in the winter. The first Roman houses had a fire in the centre of the main room. It seems they were troubled by smoke because "atrium", the Roman term for living room, has an etymology connected with "smoke escape passageway". By the end of the 3rd century the Romans had perfected their still famous central heating system: the hypocaust. This involved a fireplace below the main house whose flue passed through a series of channels underneath the floor before being diverted up chimneys in the walls. The channels could be run under the floors of several rooms giving a central heating effect with one fire heating the whole house. The system is closely analogous to the modern-day masonry heater (see

---

* Alison Kelly. The Book of English Fireplaces. Hamlyn Publishing, Feltham, Middlesex. 1968

chapter 5) and it is likely that it shared the same virtues of clean burning, convenience, and thermally efficiency. It is probable that the fire was not burned continuously but once or twice per day and the heat produced stored in the masonry surrounding the flue channels. Even by today's standards this was a good solution to the problem of heating a building. In spite of their low technology, masonry heaters achieve efficiencies as high as the best modern solid fuel burning stoves. As with so much of their technology, once the Romans withdrew from northern Europe the ability to maintain and deploy their ideas was rapidly lost.

Certain Roman remains in Britain suggest that they also used open fireplaces against walls though little is known of their design or indeed their function. Fireplaces are structures above floor level and the only thing to have survived in most cases is the hearth and occasionally the outline of a fireback. What is clear is that by the 4th century they were located against a wall and not in the centre of the room. We can only surmise what the arrangements for the fireback and chimney were. These fireplaces may have had ceremonial or religious roles but it seems likely that they were used primarily for heating though as heaters they would have been considerably less sophisticated than the hypocaust system. Following the withdrawal of Rome from northern Europe, even this level of sophistication was lost and not again achieved until the 14th century some thousand years later.

Little evidence remains about architectural practices in northern Europe and the British Isles in the centuries following the fall of the Western Roman Empire. It seems that fireplace technology reverted to the level of bonfires within two or three generations. Anglo-Saxon buildings were made of wood and none have survived but accounts tell of single story round halls built on the bare earth with central fires who's smoke escaped through a hole in the roof.

The move of fireplaces back to the wall began in the 11th and 12th centuries in Britain when the ruling class (the Norman conquerors) abandoned wooden stockades in favour of stone built castles as their main defence and residence. These castles were multi-story buildings so central fires on the ground floor would have been problematic because of the need to build a chimney through the centre of the floors above. Fires located in the centre of upper stories would lead to difficulties because upper floors were constructed from wood. Substantial stone hearths would have had to be incorporated into the wood requiring considerable engineering complexity and a fire risk would still persist. Fireplaces consequently moved to the edges of rooms.

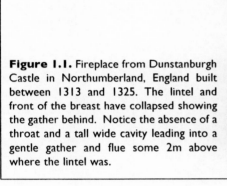

Figure 1.1. Fireplace from Dunstanburgh Castle in Northumberland, England built between 1313 and 1325. The lintel and front of the breast have collapsed showing the gather behind. Notice the absence of a throat and a tall wide cavity leading into a gentle gather and flue some 2m above where the lintel was.

Norman castles were built with walls 2m or more thick and early fireplaces were simply hollowed out of them. The earliest to survive in Britain seem to be those of Colchester Castle dating from around 1090. These comprise simple ellipsoid hollows with crude chimneys measuring 8 feet in length and serving only to divert the smoke from the fireplace to the outside by the shortest convenient route.

Castle Headington dating from 1140 has a considerably more sophisticated example of a wall based fireplace with something more akin to a chimney. By the 14th century wall based fireplaces very similar to modern designs had become common. Figures 1.1 and 1.2 show examples from Dunstanburgh Castle in Northumberland.

The great thickness of Norman Castle walls allowed them to accommodate the depth of a fireplace but this was exceptional. Most dwelling walls since then have not been so thick. Fireplaces moved into the room requiring the provision of a formal hearthstone and breast; or fireplace and chimney structures projecting from the outside of the building.

Central fires remained in use for most of the population long after the first wall based examples appeared but little data exists on how long

Figure 1.2. Another fireplace from Dunstanburgh castle, this one with the lintel in tact. It is deep, narrow and low, characteristic of pre-Rumford fireplaces. Little changed until the end of the 18th century and many modern fireplaces have reverted to this type of design!

for. The penetration of glazed windows into house construction in the 13th century must have greatly improved heat retention and made it possible to sit further from the fire in comfort making wall fires more attractive. Glazing was only available for the rich but even in their dwellings central fires continued to be built at least in small numbers to a surprisingly late date. An example at Penshurst Place in Kent dates from the mid 14th century.

The idea of central fireplaces in large rooms has never entirely died and has its modern incarnation in the form of multiple face fireplaces and fire pits. These designs employ an inverted funnel shaped canopy above the fire to catch the smoke and direct it up the chimney (figure 3.15). Some of the surviving medieval central hearths may have originally used the same idea but the canopies have not survived. Whether they ever existed and if so when they were installed remains a matter of conjecture.

It appears that the development of fireplace and chimney design between the 11th and 15th centuries was focused on minimising the rain and weather that came into the building via the chimney rather than on preventing the fire from smoking. Chimneys of this period were wide and usually had a small roof over the top. The smoke escaped through vents below the roof. They were low, not usually projecting higher that the highest point of the roof. It seems that by the 16th century it was realised that if the chimney projected substantially above the highest part of the roof it was less liable to downdrafts created by the interaction of wind with the roof.

A note in a 14th century London ordinance decrees that chimneys should be constructed of non-flammable materials such as stone or tile and no longer be constructed of wood. It seems that such chimneys consisted of a wooden frame with a lath and plaster type lining so that smoke did not come into direct contact with the wood. No known examples of this kind of chimney survive to date! It was not until the 16th century that brick became available, which is in large part why few chimneys dating from before then have survived.

Up until the end of the 16th century wood was the principal fuel used for heating in the British Isles. It started to become scarce at the beginning of the 17th century and coal imported by sea began to take over. This change in fuel brought about the redesign of fireplaces which could now be smaller but had to be equipped with the tools necessary for coal handling. After the fire of London of 1666 a vast rebuild was carried out in stone. Many more rooms were provided with fireplaces and this trend continued and led to the widespread pollution of British Victorian towns.

From the mid 16th to the early 17th centuries there was a vogue for astonishingly elaborate and verbose mantelpieces and chimney breasts which had nothing to do with the technicalities of fire functioning but afford fertile ground for historians of art, taste and design.

Approximately a century after Britain, the east cost of America also began to suffer wood shortages raising the demand for efficiency in fireplaces. Literary sources record that fireplaces of the 17th and 18th centuries were very prone to filing the room with smoke and both of these factors seem to have prompted two Americans to undertake detailed studies of fireplace designs with a view to improving them. One of these was the politician and scientist Benjamin Franklin who is credited with the development of dampers - metal plates that can be moved to adjust the size of the fire throat and limit the amount of hot air going up the chimney. He also described the 3 stages of burning wood: water, volatiles and charcoal described further in chapter 9.

The other American, who made an even greater contribution, was Count Rumford. Rumford was born as Benjamin Thomson in 1753 in Massachusetts and published a treaties on fireplaces in 1795.[†]

[†] Thompson, Benjamin. *"Of Chimney Fireplaces, with Proposals for improving them to save Fuel; to render Dwelling-houses more Comfortable and Salubrious, and effectually to prevent Chimneys from Smoking"* London 1795

Rumford developed his ideas via experimentation, trial and error. He proposed a design of fireplace that has survived as a standard to date (detailed in chapter 3). He worked very successfully in England upgrading the fireplaces of the rich and famous around the turn of the 19th century.

He owed his success to his introduction of two features: narrow throats which effectively isolated fireplaces from chimney downdrafts (see chapter 2) and firebacks specifically designed to be heated by the flames and radiate the heat into the room.

Rumford cracked the problem of fireplace design. Numerous complications have been developed since then but none has stuck and two centuries after his treaties was published his design remains about the best available for attractive efficient fires that do not smoke.

Fireplace development did not end in 1795. Rumford's design was popular and many were installed but in its original form it takes up quite a large wall area. Derivatives were developed to be narrower and deeper allowing large fires to be burned in a smaller space. Sloping firebacks were added to improve efficiency. This was a logical extension of Rumford's idea of the heated fireback. By sloping the back forward more of the flame played upon it thus heating it more than a vertical back. Rumford tried this variant himself but used it vary rarely. It was adopted with increasing frequency in later years and became more common than the original vertical back. These changes were evolutionary rather than revolutionary and fires built before the Second World War bore a recognisable resemblance to Rumford's originals.

With the introduction of techniques for studying fluid flow dynamics it became possible to examine the behaviour of fireplaces in greater detail than Rumford had been able to do. Such research carried out in the 1930s refined Rumford's ideas and corrected some errors he made but did not materially change his principles.

Just as fluid flow modelling techniques allowed fireplace performance to be optimised central heating became available. Installation costs were high for early systems but they were cheaper to run, more convenient and more effective than open fires. In Britain central heating began to become popular as the main form of domestic heating in the 1930s. By 1956, when the first clean air act was passed, most newly built houses were heated this way. The fashion of the time was to board up fireplaces in old houses and not install them in new ones. This trend seems to have been associated with architects and builders becoming deskilled in fireplace design and construction. The majority of fireplaces installed since the middle of the 20th century are of a poor standard with designs similar to those that predated Rumford's improvements. Frustration at the poor performance of modern fireplaces as found in New England stimulated a Vermont resident named Vrest Orton to write a book called "The Forgotten Art of Building a Good Fireplace"[‡]. This book was technically limited in its scope but it started a slow but sustained comeback in the popularity of Rumford's design.

With the change to central heating came a change in the temperature we expect in our buildings. It is not practical to heat a dwelling in Britain through winter to the standard we now expect using open fires alone. In spite of this, open fires are currently enjoying a rise in popularity as decorative items that yield a psychological "warmth" as well as physical heat.

The big development since the 1970s has been the technical improvement and rapidly increasing popularity of living flame type gas fires. Those made to look like solid fuel burning fires have become extremely realistic and more innovative designs have allowed gas fires to become very decorative features in their own right. So popular have they become that we are now back in a situation where few houses in the UK are built without a fireplace!

Appliances

The grates, stoves, andirons and baskets that hold the burning fuel are referred to as appliances. Details of their history are even scarcer than those of fireplaces as they tended not survive as well as the masonry structures that surrounded them. Early fireplaces both of the room centre and wall type used andirons. These have remained largely unchanged since Roman times and are still in use today.

Andirons are not suitable for burning coal and in Britain they began to give way to the grate in the 17th century when coal imports started to replace wood as the principal domestic fuel. Many early fireplaces were originally designed to house andirons and have been upgraded to house grates.

---

‡ Vrest Orton. *The Forgotten Art of Building a Good Fireplace. Hood & Co. Chambersburg PA.* 1969 ISBN 0-911469-17-6

Aside from this minor change in appliance use, development of designs focused more on the needs of cooking than heating. Many surviving medieval fireplaces were designed to burn wood and roast whole animals. The meat roasting spit was an important feature of medieval appliance technology. Early models were turned by hand but by the latter half of the 16th century clockwork operated mechanisms were available for the task. Dr Caius of Gonville and Caius College, Cambridge makes reference to a type of dog bred specially for the purpose of running in a hamster like cage rigged up to the spit turning mechanism. Interestingly Thomas Rowlandson drew a picture of a kitchen interior in South Wales depicting such a dog as late as the beginning of the 19th century. While the development of fireplace appliances was largely driven by the needs of cooking, domestic fireplaces were not equipped with ovens in large numbers until comparatively late. Pies were being made at home and send out to the Baker to bake until the 19th century.

Iron firebacks were introduced in the 14th century following the introduction of iron casting technology to medieval Britain. They were intended to protect fireplaces from heat but also acted as radiators though not as effectively as the masonry firebacks later proposed by Rumford who thought that stone or brick was better for the purpose than iron.

The fireplace in the 21st century

Open fireplaces were completely eclipsed by the introduction of central heating systems in the first half of the 20th century. Even the early coal fired central heating systems were more convenient, clean, efficient, and effective. The recently rekindled popularity of open fires has nothing to do with heating performance. They are popular because we find them attractive to look at and listen to. It is true that the heat they radiate is pleasant but radiant gas fires radiate more heat and there has been no renaissance in their popularity! Open fireplaces should be regarded as items of decoration. They do not compete in the heating appliance market. They compete effectively in the interior decor market.

By far the commonest mistake made when choosing fireplaces stems from a failure to acknowledge this fact. For some reason is felt to be unworthy to be found wanting a fireplace purely as a decoration. How often do people decide they want a fireplace and consult a catalogue or showroom where they see a design that they like, offered for a reasonable cost? A salesman or perhaps an installation engineer is consulted and starts pointing out the poor performance of what they've chosen. Reluctant to acknowledge that they are interested in beauty not heat, they are persuaded to purchase a more expensive and less attractive creation often involving glazed doors that close in front of the fire. They are reassured that you can always burn the fire with the doors open but once the thing is installing and the money spent it turns out that it doesn't draw properly with a doors open, the firebox is deep and narrow so that the fire cannot be seen well and is quite likely to keep going out unless the doors are closed. It turns out to be unsatisfactory as a decoration and as a heater and is never used!

For some the decorative appeal of an open fire is enough that they wish to enjoy one whatever the weather. The heat produced can become an undesirable byproduct in hot weather and air conditioning may be used to keep the room at a comfortable temperature while the fire is burning. This practice, found in the warmer parts of the USA, is not an indulgent folly but rather reflects an accurate understanding of the purpose of open fires. Folly is to want a fireplace but install some unattractive iron or glass fronted stove and so achieve neither an attractive fire nor a convenient heater!

Chapter 2

Draft

The term "draft" refers to the air that a fire draws in from the surrounding area. It is drawn in to fill the partial vacuum left by rising hot gases. The draft of fires can be increased with the use of a chimney which isolates the rising gases from the surrounding air allowing them to rise further before cooling. The amount of draft can be calculated with reference to figure 2.1 where a house, fire and chimney are shown together with an analogous electric circuit. Air is driven round this circuit by the buoyancy of hot gases in the chimney. This driving force can be expressed as a pressure: draft pressure. The space inside a chimney is known as the flue. When a chimney draws in this way it is said to have a "natural draft flue" to distinguish from other type of flue such as balanced flues.

Chimneys draw because hot air rises. Air expands when heated so that less mass can fit into the same space. This means that the density of air in a chimney 5m tall over a fire is less that in the same 5m outside of the chimney. The pull of gravity on the lower density air is lower so the pressure at the bottom of the chimney is lower than outside at the same level. Draft pressure is the amount by which it is lower in the theoretical situation where flow through the chimney is zero. It is simply the difference in the mass of gas in a column H high and unit area ($1m^2$) in cross section inside and outside the chimney.

The accurate way of calculating draft pressure would be to integrate the density of gases up the chimney but it is simpler and adequate for our purposes to estimate an average density. If we make the assumption that the average chemical mass of the molecules in the chimney is the same as those of the air then the density is inversely proportional to the temperature of the gas in Kelvin (K)*. A typical flue gas temperature is 300 °C (=573K). At this temperature flue gas will have roughly half the density

---

* See chapter 11 for a discussion of the different temperature scales.

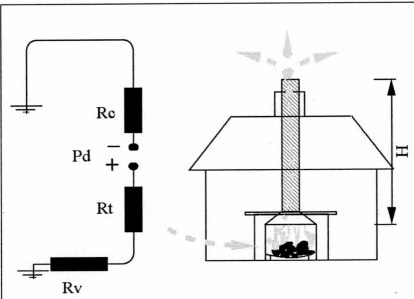

Figure 2.1. Air circulation of an open fire and an analogous electric circuit where Vd represents the draft pressure, Rc the resistance to smoke flow of the chimney, Rt the resistance of the throat and Rv the resistance to air flow of the building's ventilation system.

of air outside at about 10 °C (283K). Air at atmospheric pressure and 10°C weighs about 1.25kg/m3 so the flue gas is about .625kg/m3 lighter.

This leads to a draft pressure in a 5m chimney of 31.25 Pa[†]; not very much compared with atmospheric pressure of around 101,000 Pa but enough to drive the smoke up the chimney. The flow through the system can now be expressed as the draft pressure divided by the total resistance of the system. From the electrical analogy this is Vd/(Rc + Rt + Rv). Using the same terms for air flow and electrical resistance and Pd for draft pressure this becomes

Gas flow in the chimney = Pd/(Rc + Rt + Rv).

As Rt is raised from 0 upwards two things change. The total resistance of the circuit increases and the proportion of that resistance made up by Rt also increases. This in turn means that the total flow rate

---

† The Pascal (Pa) is the SI unit of pressure. One Pa is equal to 1N/m2

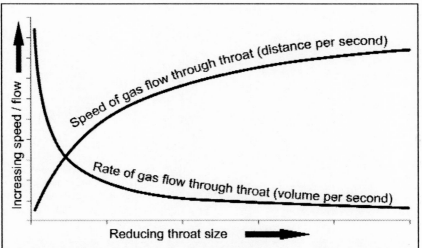

Figure 2.2. Graph showing how speed of gas movement and total flow rate in a fireplace throat change with reducing throat size. The effects of increasing chimney temperature by restricting tramp air flow and increasing throat resistance are allowed for.

through the system reduces but the pressure drop across the throat increases so the speed (in m/s) of air flowing through the throat increases (as opposed to the flow rate in m³/s which is reduced). An additional factor comes into play as Rt is raised. When the flow rate is reduced by raising the resistance of the throat, the rate of flow of the hot gases coming off the fire remain unchanged unless the throat gets very narrow, but the flow rate of cool "tramp air" flowing in over the fire from the room is reduced. This means that the hot gases are less diluted by the cool air and the chimney runs hotter, increasing the draft pressure. These two mechanisms combine to mean that reducing the throat size leads to a marked increase in the speed of gas passing the throat. This speed increase encourages laminar rather than turbulent flow. Figure 2.2 illustrates the two relationships: between throat size and flow rate and between throat size and flow speed. In practice the second mechanism of raising the chimney temperature is the most important.

There are two means by which unthroated fires smoke, the main one being downdrafts. These are gusts of wind that blow down the chimney. In an unthroated fire they briefly reverse the flow of smoke in the chimney and puff smoke that was heading up the chimney into the room. The value of high speed laminar flow through the throat is that the gas moving fast

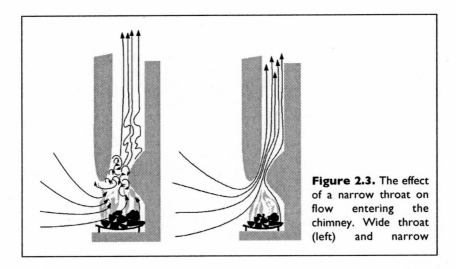

Figure 2.3. The effect of a narrow throat on flow entering the chimney. Wide throat (left) and narrow

in a uniform direction has enough momentum to resist reversal by downdrafts. The difference between slow turbulent flow in a wide throat and fast laminar flow in a narrow one is illustrated in figure 2.3.

Experiments on Draft

The best known experimenters in this area were the Americans Count Rumford and Benjamin Franklin. They based their analysis on observing the response of smoke flow to changing various fireplace design parameters. Rumford performed the most extensive study of the two and formed the following conclusions:

1) The flue should include a narrow throat just above the fireplace opening.

2) Cold air flows down the back of the chimney while warm air from the fire flows up the front (figure 2.4). In this Rumford was mistaken.

3) This draft of cold air causes smoking when it meets the upcoming air from the fire (figure 2.4).

4) A smoke shelf is needed to deflect the upcoming air back up the chimney and avoid it meeting smoke "head on" (figure 2.4).

These last three points were wrong but the the idea of a narrow throat was correct and so successful that overall Rumford's designs

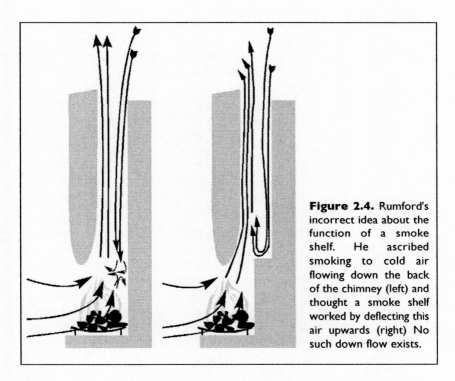

Figure 2.4. Rumford's incorrect idea about the function of a smoke shelf. He ascribed smoking to cold air flowing down the back of the chimney (left) and thought a smoke shelf worked by deflecting this air upwards (right) No such down flow exists.

worked well despite the redundancy, and indeed counter productiveness, of the smoke shelf.

Rumford developed his principles of fireplace design by trial and error. Some features of his designs were constrained by the existing masonry he worked with (most of his work was in rebuilding existing fireplaces) and some by the practices of the time. Chimneys then were wide and had no throat. Rumford was not able to narrow whole chimneys partly because of expense and partly because access for small boys had to be allowed for sweeping. He thus narrowed only the throat but still had to allow small boy access. He solved this problem by introducing removable bricks and this is probably where the smoke shelf idea originated.

The success of Rumford's ideas is undeniable but without access to the fluid flow modeling methods of later years he had no way of telling exactly which features of his design contributed. He was inclined to think that each feature was important and it appears that he developed his theory of cold air flowing down the back of the chimney because it fitted with his belief about the smoke shelf. Smoke is visible and reasonable conclusions can follow from simple observation of fires. Rumford had extensive experience of a design of fireplace and wide chimney which is now very rarely seen. We must therefore concede that Rumford's theory may just possibly have been correct and his smoke shelf may have worked the way he thought in the particular type of fireplaces with which he was familiar. Fluid flow analysis of fireplaces since that time shows that even if Rumford's idea was correct for fires of his age (which is very doubtful) it is not correct for modern narrower chimney fires but the idea refuses to die. It was extolled by Orton in his book "The Forgotten Art of Building a Good Fireplace" and has been regurgitated by masonry books ever since.

Probably the best known experimental results since Rumford and Frankiln are those of P.O. Rosin. Rosin was commissioned by interests representing the British coal industry to investigate draft and optimal fireplace design. Beginning work in the 1930s his aim was to define the characteristics of air flow associated with open fires including flow in the room, fireplace and chimney. He used a physical water based model of fluid flow. Slowly moving water behaves in a closely analogous way to slowly moving air at a roughly constant pressure and this allows conclusions about one system (air in a fireplace) to be drawn from observations on the other (water in the model).

It is possible to build a water model and simply heat the water at a point corresponding to the fire grate. The warmer water would expand, become less dense and rise up the model's chimney. An alternative approach is to add something to the water at the grate to make it more dense so it sinks, and then turn the model upside down so that the sinking water flows down the chimney. This can be done by placing a block of salt in the grate. The salt dissolves in the water making it more dense as it leaves the grate area. This was the method used by Rosin. He built a ¼ scale model of a fireplace in clear plastic. He mounted this upside down in a tank of water. In the grate where the fire burns he placed a coloured salt block. The flow of water was then observed by injecting streams of dye with fine needles at various points and observing the flow of coloured dye away from the needles and coloured salt block. Bizarre as it sounds, this system reproduces the air flow round a fireplace remarkably accurately except for one important aspect: downdrafts. A real fire installation has to contend with random gusts of air blowing down the chimney. Rosin was not able to accurately reproduce this phenomenon and his conclusions, while true, were somewhat idealised.

Rosin's principle findings were:

1) The combustion gases cling closely to the back of the flue contradicting Rumford's theory (which lay behind the smoke shelf idea). This finding was consistent across a range of throat and fireback configurations. The effect was most marked with large tramp air flows but would fail if laminar flow was totally disrupted by turbulence in the chimney.

2) Streaming of combustion gases up the back of the flue leads to stratification with hot gases at the back of the chimney which is often on an outside wall and so the heat they give to the wall is largely wasted. Cold tramp air streams up the front side of the chimney directly behind the breast where heat could be usefully transferred to the room were the gases hot!

3) If a smoke shelf is used then considerable turbulence is generated above it.

4) Turbulent eddies of air flow close to the fire opening lead to smoking. Rosin found such eddies in two locations as shown in figure 2.5. The higher one is caused by the smoke shelf which is not recommended because of this result. This eddy is usually far

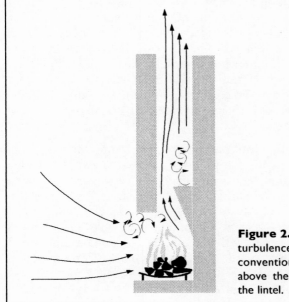

Figure 2.5. Two main locations of turbulence found by Rosin in conventional fireplaces designs: above the smoke shelf and below the lintel.

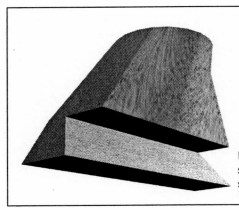

Figure 2.6. The shape of the smoke spaces above a fire using a smoke shelf.

enough up the chimney to pose little risk of spilling into the room. The main problem is the eddies created around the lintel.

5) By narrowing the throat, air flow through it is speeded up. This creates a one way valve effect. Once throat action is established no smoke will pass down through it. It may well billow up and down the chimney but will not breach the throat because of the momentum of gases moving in the other direction.

Putting these points noted in an idealised system into a realistic context, smoking is caused by a combination if turbulent air flow close to the fireplace opening and downdrafts from the chimney pot. All chimneys suffer some random downdrafts caused by changing wind conditions around the pot. Turbulent eddies close to the lintel are easily blown into the room by such downdrafts. If however fast laminar flow can be established in the area just above the fire opening, i.e. in the throat, then it is much more difficult for downdrafts to disrupt and spill smoke into the room.

Rosin investigated the drafting properties of numerous designs of fireplace and experimentally determined the design features which minimized eddy formation. These are: using a narrow throat, making the lintel, fireback and throat smooth and aerodynamic, avoiding sharp edges particularly of hoods and avoiding a smoke shelf. Rosin suggested that the flue cross section should be reduced to 125-200cm². He based this on the observation that if laminar flow can be maintained all the way up the chimney then its resistance is markedly reduced and also that the expansion above the throat causes eddies. This is all very well if laminar flow is maintained which it may not be. It is safer to use

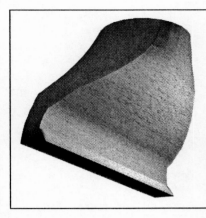

Figure 2.7. The shape of the flue in an improved throat. The gather and throat is smooth as is the re-expansion into the bottom of the flue.

a larger chimney that will still function if laminar flow is disrupted. This is assumed in the building regulations.

A consequence of the smoke shelf idea is the smoke chamber, a cavity above the smoke shelf which narrows into the chimney proper giving a double gather effect as shown in figure 2.6. A much better throat is illustrated in figure 2.7. A conventional damper is a hinged plate that allows the size of the throat opening to be varied in order to minimise tramp air flow. It causes similar turbulence to a smoke shelf and rather spoils laminar flow. Chimney top dampers do not have this problem and work equally well but require a more elaborate system of control.

Because the smoke shelf remains prevalent in text books and articles about fireplace construction you may understandably be reluctant to accept dismissal of it. It is not an issue of great importance because the smoke shelf may not do any good but it does rather little harm. The turbulence it produces is above the throat and so will only cause the fire to smoke if its performance is otherwise marginal. The standard designs of fireplaces and chimneys provide ample draft and adding a smoke shelf is unlikely to adversely affect function in any significant way.

Tramp air and efficiency

Tramp air is the term applied to cool room air that passes up the chimney without going through the fire. Tramp air flow cools the masonry of the fireplace and reduces heat output but the main effect is the loss of warm room air and its replacement with cold outside air.

The amount of heat lost in this way is dependent on the temperature of the outside air. In subzero conditions such as are encountered during the winter in northern Europe, Canada and the northern US this heat loss can be, and frequently is, greater than the heat output of the fire. This is how fires can have "negative efficiency". The difficulty of heating a house with an open fire in such circumstances led to the development of the Masonry Heater.

Some tramp air flow is necessary to scavenge the air around the fire and draw stray wisps of smoke into the chimney. In fires designed to be efficient, tramp air flow is restricted to the minimum amount compatible with preventing smoking. Such designs are geared to good performance when the fireplace and chimney are at their normal operational temperatures. Tramp air is designed to be marginal at such temperatures and with a cool chimney and consequently reduced draft it is frequently inadequate. This is why such fireplaces tend to smoke a bit when the fire has just been lit especially if it has been laid up at the front of the grate. Dampers work by adjusting the amount of tramp air flow to the minimum which prevents smoking.

Ventilation schemes

When reopening or installing an open fire some consideration must be given to room ventilation. In old houses with drafty floors and windows no additional ventilation may be needed but in more recent houses or where extensive refurbishment has been undertaken specific provision is likely to be necessary. The amount of ventilation in buildings is reckoned according to "equivalent area". A range of commercial vents is available and they vary from simple grills to more complex ducts that block out drafts and sound while allowing ventilation. The "equivalent area" quoted by manufacturers for such vents is the area of an open hole in the wall that would provide the same amount of ventilation. Building regulations in the UK require that the total equivalent ventilation area of a room with an open fire is equal to at least 50% of the area of the throat (or flue if no throat is included) and the vents must not be closable. Strictly it is not necessary to comply with when reopening an an old fireplace without extensive works like chimney relining. If substantial work is being done or if a significant change is being made to the design of the fireplace like changing the size or fuel used, then the regulations must be complied with. Even in drafty old houses formal ventilation is needed if compliance is required to show that adequate ventilation exists and also that it is not liable to being blocked by future common alterations such as carpeting or replacing windows.

Installers should position vents to minimise the chances of their becoming blocked either accidentally or deliberately to stop noise or drafts. The worst place to put them is at ground level far away from the fire because cold air flowing in will not mix with the warmer room air (because it is more dense) and will create cold drafts around people's legs. It is better to put them high up on walls or ceilings far away from the fire. This will give even mixing of room and ventilation air but will increase ventilatory heat loss. Best is to place the vents on the wall around the fire. The cold inflowing air then goes straight up the chimney without cooling the room air or causing drafts where occupants are sitting. Such positioning is rarely practicable and placing them in the floor around the hearth is virtually as good and much easier.

Extractor fans

Open fires do not mix well with extractor fans which lower the pressure in a building and can easily disrupt or even reverse flow in a chimney. A rough figure of 31 Pa is calculated above for draft pressure and a powerful extractor fan can reduce the pressure by more than this amount. Control systems for extractor fans used to regulate the pressure in buildings typically maintain a negative pressure of 15 to 20 Pa. Where an extractor fan is installed in the same building as an open fire, the fire must be able to operate satisfactorily while it is running at its highest setting. Small extractor fans in the building but not in the same room as the fire generally present little problem. Fans in the same room need extra care. A fire that draws well can tolerate a fan in the same room with a modest negative pressure of 10 to 15 Pa but to guarantee this requires that the room is well ventilated (with vents other than the fan!), that the fan is small (20l/min flow or less) or that we use pressure regulating control system which turns the fan off if the pressure sensor fails.

Venting to high pressure zones

It is occasionally feasible to solve an otherwise difficult drafting problem due to the chimney top being in a high pressure zone by venting the room to the same zone. At its simplest this involves installing a vent on the windward wall of a building. More complex ducting systems can connect the room to a more remote area. Placing the vent inlet close to the chimney pot stands a good chance of adequately equalising the pressures but siphoning is a potential risk (see chapter 7). This will only work if the room's ventilation is wholly or mainly via the duct. In drafty old buildings you are not likely to achieve this with a long ducting system. Limitations of this kind of ventilation are the installation expense and the difficulty of predicting if it will solve the problem. If possible you should try a makeshift system first.

———————————

Chapter 3

Fireplaces

There are two ways in which smoke from an autumn bonfire moves sideways and not up. The main one is by light wind blowing billowing turbulent smoke. Close inspection of the smoke coming off a briskly burning bonfire reveals that immediately above the flames, smoke flows in fast, vertical or near vertical streams. This is laminar flow. Even in windy conditions this area of laminar flow does not deviate much from vertical. Within at most a few feet, frequently a few inches, this laminar flow is replaced by billowing turbulent flow. In contrast to the stability of the fast laminar smoke this turbulently swirling smoke is easily blown almost horizontally and into eyes by a light breeze.

The second cause of sideways movement of smoke is the random spurts of flame and smoke which shoot out of burning fuels such as wood.

Fires in fireplaces behave in the same way as bonfires if not constrained by the fireplace design. Two methods are used to prevent smoke from getting into the room. The first and universally applied method is scavenging. This is the drawing of air from around the fire into the chimney without it passing through the fire. Scavenging ensures that any smoke that gets into the scavenged area immediately around the fire will go up the chimney and not into the room. Air flowing up the chimney without passing through the fire (tramp air) is responsible for scavenging. The scavenged area is enlarged by increasing tramp air flow and this in turn is done by widening the opening between the fire box and chimney - the throat. Scavenging is also improved by decreasing the size of the fireplace opening because there is then less area that has to be scavenged. Fireplaces that rely on scavenging to prevent smoke from entering the room are thus low, deep and narrow with little or no throat (figure 3.1). Such fireplaces are unattractive and inefficient. Unattractive because the low opening means little of the fire can be seen from the room and inefficient because the high tramp air flow draws a lot of cold air into the room and increases the ventilatory heat loss up the chimney. Moreover the

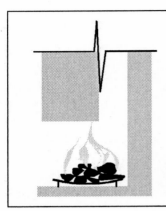

Figure 3.1. Typical cross section of a fireplace that depends on scavenging to prevent smoking. Not recommended.

low opening reduces the amount of radiant heat reaching the room from the fire and fireback.

The second method of preventing smoke from getting into the room is the basis of all well designed fireplaces. It is to encourage and maintain laminar flow of smoke well into the chimney and so eliminate the problem of turbulent unstable smoke. Scavenging can then be restricted to the smallest amount compatible with gathering up all the odd wisps of smoke emanating from the fire. This second method was introduced and perfected by Count Rumford at the end of the 18th century.

Unlike bonfires, fireplaces are generally inside rooms and built against one wall. They are not subject to wind blowing across them taking billowing smoke with it. They smoke when gusts of wind blow down the chimney. Just as fast laminar flowing smoke is stable and resists sideways deflection it also resists being stopped or reversed because of the momentum of fast flowing gases. Laminar flowing gas acts as a one way valve, preventing gusts blowing smoke down into the room.

You achieve fast laminar flow by designing a smooth funnel shape called a "gather" above the flames leading to a narrow throat. The chimney draws the rising smoke through this narrowing so that, just at the point where the smoke from a bonfire would slow down and billow, the smoke from the fire is kept fast moving through a smooth channel and remains laminar (figures 2.3 and 2.7). This system so effectively prevents smoke from entering the room that the undesirable features of a fire dependent on scavenging only can be drastically reduced. The fireplace can be shallower with a much higher lintel. This is the basis of the Rumford fireplace.

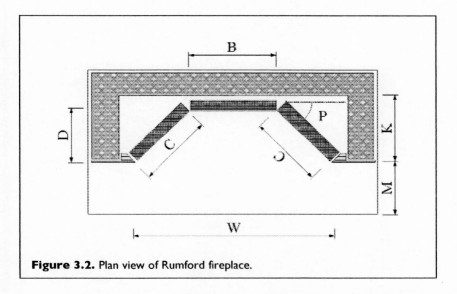

Figure 3.2. Plan view of Rumford fireplace.

Despite their poor aesthetic and thermal performance, scavenging fires are the commonest type encountered in modern houses. The reason is that they are easy to design and build. A builder with little knowledge of the subject is likely to install this type of fire even in the UK where the inset* range of fireplaces is widely available.

Rumford fires

An account of the origins of Rumford's fire design was included in chapters 1 and 2. His basic design remains a standard today for efficiency and aesthetics, in spite of which it is not often seen. Part of the reason for this seems to be historical. Open fires went out of fashion when stoves and central heating replaced them as the main form of domestic heating in the UK and USA. For a period of several decades in the last half of the 20th century very few were built and this fact coupled with the fairly exacting design and workmanship requirements for Rumford fireplaces drove them into disuse. The necessary knowledge and skill was largely lost from the building community. When an open fire was specified, a simple scavenging design was installed.

---

* "Inset" refers to a range of fireplaces that are made from manufactured components widely available in the UK. Further details of the type are given in Chapter 4.

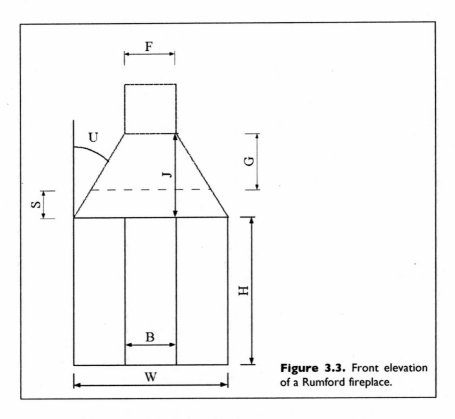

Figure 3.3. Front elevation of a Rumford fireplace.

Figures 3.2 - 3.4 show the plan, front and side elevations of a Rumford fireplace. In its basic form the fireplace opening is square. It can be made lower than it is wide by lowering the lintel but should not be made higher than the width or it will be liable to smoke especially when the chimney is cold.

Rumford's design works equally well with andirons or a grate. The shallowness of the design means that the fire is likely to come forward of the plane of the fire-surround facing, especially with andirons where the confines of the fire are less well defined. It is sensible to extend the refractory paving of the true hearth in front of the fireplace by 100 - 200mm. A large Rumford fireplace can be well over 1m wide and 350mm deep. The standard hearth extent of 500mm in front of the fireplace and 150mm to either side of the opening is modest in such cases. If building a fireplace on this scale you would be better to extend the hearth in front of the fireplace opening to not less than half the opening width.

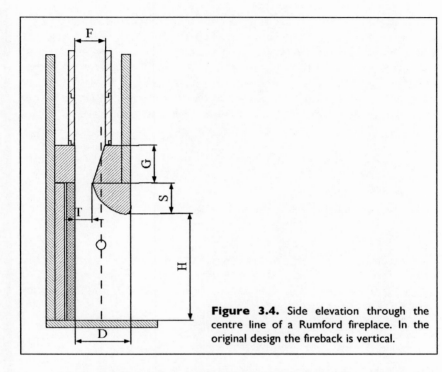

Figure 3.4. Side elevation through the centre line of a Rumford fireplace. In the original design the fireback is vertical.

The risk of logs rolling out of the fire is greater with andirons than with a grate. A hearth fender will improve safety. This is a low fireproof barrier that stands 50-100mm above the floor around the edge of the hearth. It can be a permanent construction of masonry or a movable metal structure. Its function is to stop anything rolling out of the fire before it gets to the combustible floor.

When calculating the dimensions of a fireplace first the width (W) is decided on then the other dimensions referred to in figures 3.2-3.4 can be calculated relative to W according to the following relationships:

$H = W$
$B = 0.44 \times W$
$C = 0.44 \times W$
$D = W/3$
$U = 30\text{-}45^\circ$
$K = W/3 + \text{(firebrick thickness)} + 10 \text{ to } 25mm$
$M = \text{at least } 500mm \text{ (required UK) or } W/2 \text{ if greater (recommended)}$
$P = ArcSin(D/C)^\circ$

Dimensions G, J, S, and T define the throat and gather. Prefabricated components may be used for these in which case the geometry will be defined though there may be a decision to make about the throat width. If a throat damper is to be used it will form the throat and the masonry must be designed fit it and allow space for its movement. If no damper or a flue top damper are to be used, a throat is formed with its narrowest part up to 200mm above the lintel:

S = 200mm

$$J = \frac{(W - F)}{2TanU}$$

When U = 45° Tan(U) = 1, when U = 30° Tan(U) =0.58.

G = J-S

The cross section area of the throat for a Rumford fire is smaller in proportion to the opening size than for other fires with a ratio (Q) of 1/15 to 1/20 or about half the cross section area of the flue. This gives the rather horrible formula:

$$T = \frac{W\left(1 - W/Q\right)}{2STanU}$$ or 40 mm, whichever is greater, for the layout

shown in figure 3.3 where Q is 15 for fires under 1.2m wide, 20 for those between 1.2m and 1.7m wide and 30 for those over 1.7m wide. If the throat extends across the entire width of the fireplace its width is W and this simplifies to T = W/Q. T should not be less than 40 mm.

F is the flue diameter. This can be calculated from the formula below where R is the ratio of fireplace opening area to flue area. This is 8 for most fires but can be raised to 10 for smaller Rumford fires and for very large Rumford fires can be raised considerably to 20. In practice the nearest standard size of flue liner is used.

$$F = \sqrt{4HW/\pi R}$$

These dimensions do not have to be exact and once the approximate size of a fireplace is chosen scope exists for minor variations. The precise final dimensions will probably be dictated by either the availability of preformed firebacks or the type of appliance you plan to use.

If you are installing andirons or a specially made appliance the above formulas can be applied exactly but this is likely to mean a lot of unnecessary brick cutting. It is easiest to arrange the dimensions so that they fit whole numbers of firebricks which come in two standard sizes that differ only in their thickness. They are still imperial: 9×4½×3 inches (228.6×114.3×76.2mm) and 9×4½×2½ inches (228.6×114.3×63.5mm). Firebricks are usually laid half over each other and half firebricks known as "bats" with a face size of 4½×4½ inches (114.3×114.3mm) are available. Table 3.1 gives a range of dimensions that approximate the ratios above but fit with multiples of 4½ inches plus a 4mm mortar gap. They are intended for firebacks made with standard firebricks in the shiner position.

A common variant on Rumford's design is shown in figures 3.5 and 3.6 in which the upper $^2/_3$ of the fireback slopes forwards. This makes the fireplace more efficient because the slope is heated by the flames and radiates the heat into the room. The dimensions for this type of fireback are as for Rumfords above except that the amount by which the upper $^2/_3$ slopes forwards has to be decided. It will usually be

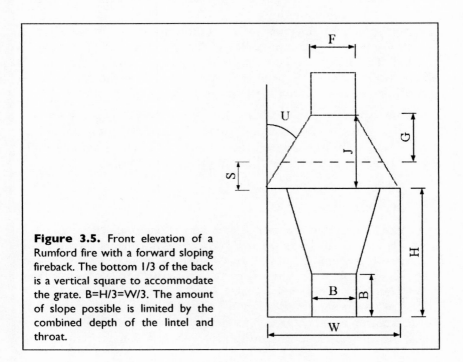

Figure 3.5. Front elevation of a Rumford fire with a forward sloping fireback. The bottom 1/3 of the back is a vertical square to accommodate the grate. B=H/3=W/3. The amount of slope possible is limited by the combined depth of the lintel and throat.

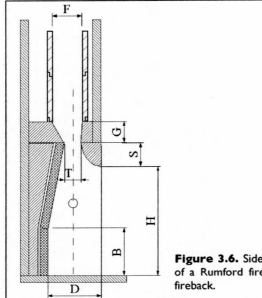

Figure 3.6. Side elevation through the middle of a Rumford fireplace with a forward sloping fireback.

determined by the thickness of the lintel and depth of the throat. Lintels are typically 100mm thick and the throat is in the range 50 to 100mm. This limits the amount of slope possible and in fires under about 700mm wide it is so little as to not be worth the trouble. For larger fires the slope should be as much as the lintel and throat allow.

Other variants are possible. One is the "Kiva" type where the fireback follows the same overall dimensions as the Rumford but is formed into a continuous curve rather than 3 or 4 flat surfaces. It is an efficient and attractive design but not the easiest to build.

Conventional fires

Rumford's design remains a standard of thermal efficiency and aesthetic appeal but in its original form the grate size is rather small compared to the amount of wall space given to the fire. Most Rumford fireplace openings are between 1m and 2m square. When the proportions of the design are scaled down to fit smaller openings the grate size becomes impractically small especially for wood burning fires. For this reason manufacturers have designed a range of small fireplaces which broadly adhere to Rumford's principles but alter the proportions

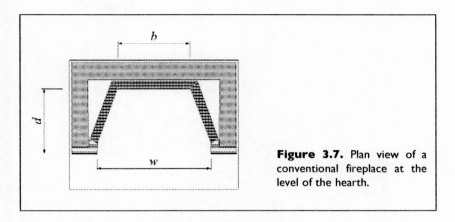

Figure 3.7. Plan view of a conventional fireplace at the level of the hearth.

to allow a larger grate size. Such fireplaces are known as conventional fires and are much more common than Rumford types in the UK.

There is no clear cut off between conventional and Rumford types. The term "Rumford fire" is used to refer to square fireplaces that are approximately three times as wide as they are deep. This represents the extreme in height and shallowness of a spectrum of serviceable designs. Figures 3.7 – 3.9 and tables 3.2 and 3.3 give the relative dimensions of conventional fireplaces. The exact geometry of this type of fireplace is not critical and a number of successful variations are possible. The main determinant is the ratio between width and depth. There is no rule on how much wider a fireplace must be than it is deep but the advantages of Rumford's design are substantially compromised if it is less than 1½ to 2 times. It is recommended that the ratio of width to depth be kept between 1½ and 3.

Because such fireplaces are common, parts for them are easily obtainable and exact dimensions are likely to be determined by what appliance is to be installed. If not tables 3.2 and 3.3 provide a number of designs which fit standard firebrick dimensions.

When designing conventional fires we first chose the width (w) and then calculate the other dimensions from w according to the following relationships:

$h=2/3$ to $1\times w$
$d=w/3$ to $w/1.5$
$e=h/2$ (not critical)
$i=$as required for damper

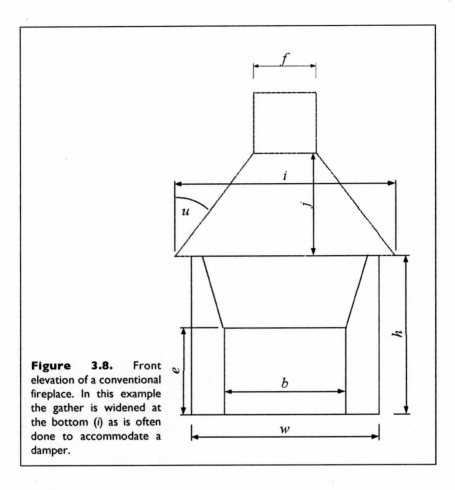

Figure 3.8. Front elevation of a conventional fireplace. In this example the gather is widened at the bottom (*i*) as is often done to accommodate a damper.

$j = (i\text{-}f)/2$
$u = 30$ to $45°$

t is as for Rumford fires except that a ratio of throat area to fireplace opening area is 1/12 to 1/16 rather than 1/15 to 1/20

No hot fireback

Now that a fireplace's primarily function is more likely to be decorative than it is to be a heating appliance the advantages of heat radiating firebacks has diminished and many fireplaces do not use them. The alternative is to have a grate or andirons in what amounts to

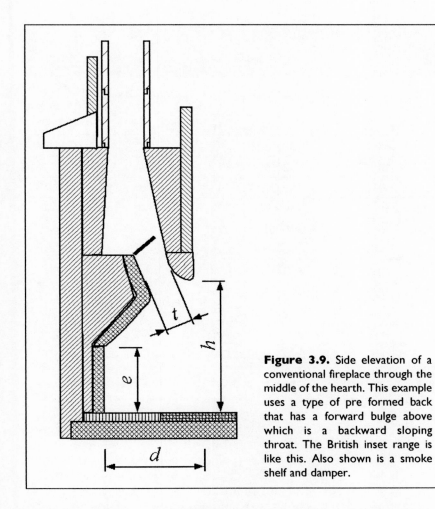

Figure 3.9. Side elevation of a conventional fireplace through the middle of the hearth. This example uses a type of pre formed back that has a forward bulge above which is a backward sloping throat. The British inset range is like this. Also shown is a smoke shelf and damper.

a rough opening below a gather and throat. This is a retreat from the technically superior designs outlined above but offers an appearance that blends well with rustic or natural architectural styles. Frank Lloyd Wright frequently employed this kind of fireplace in association with interior bare brick or riven stone and his ideas have been widely copied.

The opening of a fireplace like this is large with a substantial paved area acting as the true hearth. The fire can be located in the middle of this area and need not be built up against a wall. This means that while the hearth should be paved with refractory material there is no need to construct the rough opening from firebricks.

Table 3.1. Dimensions of different sizes of Rumford fireplace in mm assuming standard firebricks of 228.6×114.3mm (9×4½ inches) and a 4mm thickness of cement

B		C		W	D	H		Angle	Flue
Brick lengths	mm	Brick lengths	mm			Brick wythes	mm	U °	diameter approx
1	233	1	233	533	178	4	473	40	175-190
2	349	1	233	594	198	5	592	32	190-230
1	233	2	349	732	244	6	710	46	230
2	349	2	349	799	266	7	828	40	290
2	465	2	349	862	287	7	828	35	300
2	349	2	465	999	333	8	946	44	350
2	465	2	465	1066	355	9	1065	40	350
3	698	3	698	1599	533	13	1538	40	500
3	698	4	930	1998	666	17	2011	44	500
4	930	3	698	1723	574	15	1775	35	500
4	930	4	930	2132	711	18	2129	40	500

Dimensions in mm. To convert to inches divide by 25.4

For fireplaces of this type of up to about 1200mm wide and 400mm deep the design is fairly straightforward. The flue diameter is calculated as 1/8 to 1/10 of the area of the fireplace opening. The lintel should not be more than twice as high as the fireplace is deep. A gather rises behind the lintel at not more than 45° to the vertical and is narrowed to a smooth throat with a minimum cross section area of 50 – 70% of the flue if no throat damper is used. Aerodynamic design is not as critical as with Rumford fireplaces and a standard flat bottomed lintel and corbeled gather usually work. The fireplace shown in figure 6.4 is of this type.

The design becomes more difficult and behavior less predictable for fireplaces larger than 1200mm wide. The reason is that when fireplace size is scaled up it is not usually to accommodate a larger fire but rather for decorative reasons or to accommodate things within the rough opening such as fuel, fire irons or cooking utensils.

b		c		W	d		h		Angle	Flue
Brick lengths	mm	Brick lengths	mm		Brick wythes	mm	Brick wythes	mm	u °	diameter approx.
1	233	1.5	349	745	2	237	6	710	47	230
1	233	2	465	834	3	355	7	828	40	300
1.5	349	2	465	950	3	355	8	946	40	300
2	465	2	465	1067	3	355	9	1065	40	400
2	465	2.5	582	1141	4	473	10	1183	36	400
2.5	582	2.5	582	1257	4	473	10	1183	36	400
3	698	2.5	582	1374	4	473	11	1301	36	500
3.5	814	2.5	582	1490	4	473	12	1420	36	500
2	465	3	698	1206	5	592	10	1183	32	400
2.5	582	3	698	1322	5	592	11	1301	32	400
3	698	3	698	1438	5	592	12	1420	32	500
3.5	814	3	698	1555	5	592	13	1538	32	500
4	930	3	698	1671	5	592	14	1656	32	500
4.5	1047	3	698	1787	5	592	15	1775	32	500
2.5	582	3.5	814	1700	5	592	15	1775	43	500
3	698	3.5	814	1817	5	592	15	1775	43	500

Table 3.2. Dimensions of different sizes of conventional fireplace assuming standard firebricks of 228.6×114.3mm (9×4½ inches) and a 4mm thickness of cement with depth specified in bricks

Dimensions in mm. To convert to inches divide by 25.4

For fireplaces that are considerably wider than they are high there will be substantial space on either side of fire. It is primarily the size of the fire in the grate rather than the area of the fireplace opening that determines the draft requirements so simple application of the ratio rule would lead to an inappropriately wide flue in this situation. An "effective open area" must therefore be estimated. This is best done by calculating

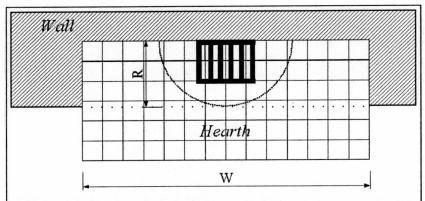

Figure 3.10. Plan view of a fireplace that is substantially wider than the fire. The effective open area is the height of the lintel times W or πR which ever is less.

the area of a cylindrical surface the same height as the lintel centered on the grate and tangential to the front of the lintel as shown in figure 3.10.

Inglenook

A true inglenook is a rough opening fireplace which is large enough to accommodate seating as well as the fire rather than a small extension to the room with a fireplace in its far wall. The opening of an inglenook must be at least 2m by 2m to accommodate this seating but the size of the fire is not enlarged in proportion. Typically a grate size of 300 by 200mm will be used and this is suited to a 230mm flue diameter with a cross sectional area of about 0.04m². Applying the ratio rule of 1/10 gives an opening size of 0.4m², one tenth of the requirement. Increasing the flue size won't help as it leads to a "flue too large for the fire" problem as discussed in chapter 7. As with the wide fire mentioned above the effective opening does not extend across the whole width but it does involve the whole height to the lintel. Because of this mismatch between fireplace and fire size a true inglenook system draws very poorly and smokes – a lot. The problem is got round either by installing a fire in the back wall which rather spoils the effect of an inglenook or by reducing the effective height to the lintel. This can be done by a combination of raising the hearth and putting in a hood. The ratio rule can be stretched to around 1/12 if the inglenook has no drafty windows or floor gaps because the air current is directed along the inglenook towards the fire by the narrow low space and this reduces smoking.

Table 3.3. **Dimensions of different sizes of conventional fireplace assuming standard firebricks of 228.6×114.3mm (9×4½ inches) and a 4mm thickness of cement with depth specified in mm**

b		*c*		*w*	*d*	*h*		Angle	Flue
Brick lengths	mm	Brick lengths	mm			Brick wythes	mm	u o	diameter
1	233	1	233	470	200	4	473	31	175 - 190
1.5	349	1	233	586	200	5	592	31	176 - 190
1.5	349	1.5	349	705	300	6	710	31	177 - 190
2	465	1.5	349	821	300	7	828	31	190
1.5	349	2	465	824	400	8	946	31	230
2	465	2	465	940	400	9	1065	31	230
2.5	582	2	465	1057	400	9	1065	31	230
3	698	2	465	1173	400	9	1065	31	230

Dimensions in mm. To convert to inches divide by 25.4

Choice of fuel: Coal or Wood

Wood has a lower heat yield than coal per kg (around 18MJ v 30MJ) and is also less dense at 0.4-0.8kg/l versus around 1.3kg/l for coal. From combining these results it can be calculated that wood yields around $1/3$ the heat of coal for the same volume so wood burning fires must have larger grates for the same heat output that those burning coal. There is another consideration which makes the difference even greater. The larger fireplace size needed to burn wood calls for a larger volume of the room around the fireplace to be effectively scavenged to prevent smoking. This means a larger tramp air flow and more ventilatory heat loss. In practice wood burning fires need about twice the grate area (equates to around 3 times the "fire volume" and 1.4 times the width and depth) for the same total heat production. Overall the performance of wood burning fires is far more marginal than that of coal fires. It is easy for a wood burning fire to lose more heat in ventilatory loss than it radiates into the room and thus have negative efficiency. For a coal fire to do so is rare. Consequently wood burning fires attract a greater degree of sophistication than do coal burners. In particular wood burning fires usually have dampers fitted. In many wood burning areas such as the USA, building regulations require that dampers are fitted to all new fireplaces. In the coal burning UK we rarely bother with dampers as their benefit is much smaller.

They may not be good heaters but do not dismiss wood burning fires. Open fires are usually installed primarily as decorations and only secondarily as heating appliances. As decorations wood burners win over coal burners. Moreover they are cleaner, produce less noxious smoke, and wood is a renewable fuel.

Building a fireplace

When installing a new hearth, fireplace or chimney, or relining a chimney, you should put essential details of the installation on a permanent notice. The details should include:

- The location of the fireplace or the location of the bottom end of the flue.
- The flue category and the types of appliances that can be safely accommodated.
- The type and size of the flue or liner and the manufacturer's name.
- The date of installation.

When building a fireplace and chimney together it is recommended that a rough fire opening is built and then the chimney completed before the fireplace is finished. If the fireplace is built while the chimney is under construction or before it is built, masonry and mortar falling down the chimney may damage the fireplace, block the throat, or jam the damper if one is being used. The suggested sequence for building a fireplace from scratch is to lay the foundation footing, build the rough opening, build the complete chimney including pot and flashing and only then return to complete the true hearth, fireback, gather and throat. This sequence has a problem. The masonry around the throat conveniently supports the weight of the flue liners. If you build the chimney first you must find some means of supporting the liners until the throat is built. You can do this by installing a commercially available product like a throat forming lintel to form one side of the throat that is completed later or a concrete slab with a hole for the flue at the bottom of the chimney. Alternatively you can use a temporary support of wood or blocks. The flue liners are then stuck to the chimney walls with back filling concrete (see chapter 8) or dabs of cement. The resulting horizontal bonds will hold well enough to allow the temporary supports to be removed but will not remain sound after the repeated heat cycling of long use so the masonry around the fireback will still have to be carefully constructed to support the liners.

Foundation Footing

This is a concrete foundation slab intended to spread the load of the fireplace and chimney over a suitable area of ground. The footing must bear the weight of the fireplace and chimney and any fireplaces on upper floors using the same chimney. Its construction depends on the local geology but 300mm thick by twice the width by twice the depth of the chimney's outer dimensions is generally adequate. It should be wider if the building has more than 2 stories. In that event it should have steel re-enforcement rods places 200mm apart 100mm above the bottom of the footing. The footing should be placed low enough underground so that the bottom at least is below the frost line. This is the lowest depth that is expected to be frozen in cold weather. It varies from place to place. Local authorities and building codes detail specific depths. It is under 500mm in most of the UK but can be as deep as 2m in areas with more severe winters such as the North Eastern USA and Scandinavia.

The constructional hearth

This is the concrete slab which carries the hearth and fireplace. The footing, being laid below the frost line, will usually be too low to place the constructional hearth directly onto it. If so a rectangular brick breast must be built above the footing to carry the constructional hearth This can be built with one or two wythes of brick depending on the hearth size. It will carry the weight of the fireplace and chimney if a vertical chimney is to be used. It may contain an ash pit and clear out door. The hearth will jut out from the chimney breast into the floor of the room (figure 3.11). For this reason it needs steel reinforcement. Local building regulations prescribe the minimum thickness of the hearth and the amount by which it must jut into the room. In general a concrete slab not less than 125mm thick is used with steel reinforcement in the middle. It projects not less than 500mm in front of and 150mm to the side of the fire opening. A wooden frame and base

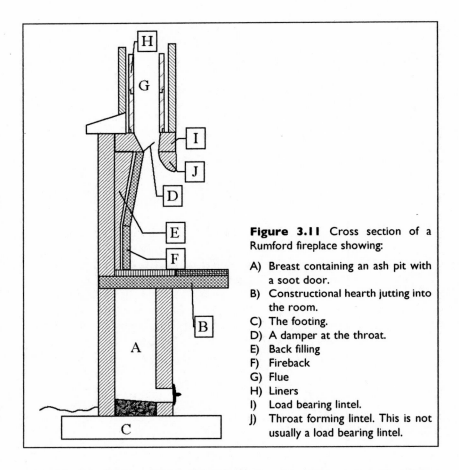

Figure 3.11 Cross section of a Rumford fireplace showing:

A) Breast containing an ash pit with a soot door.
B) Constructional hearth jutting into the room.
C) The footing.
D) A damper at the throat.
E) Back filling
F) Fireback
G) Flue
H) Liners
I) Load bearing lintel.
J) Throat forming lintel. This is not usually a load bearing lintel.

is constructed and concrete poured in. Local building codes determine whether the frame must be removed after the concrete has set but in general inaccessible parts can be left in place. The concrete should be a 1:2:3 type (ratio of Portland cement : sand : gravel – see chapter 8). Figure 3.11 shows how it is laid onto the breast masonry. If an ash pit is to be built then the constructional hearth will have to have a hole to accommodate the pit opening.

The rough opening

The rough opening is usually designed to fit around a specific firebox or appliance. If the appliance has not been specified then an opening at least 1000mm high by 800mm wide by 340mm deep should be made. Though not essential, the later construction of the firebox and throat is considerably simplified if the breast is left incomplete above the lintel or the lintel is left out above the rough opening to allow direct access to the lowest flue liner. This is particularly so if a smooth throat and gather is to be used as described below.

The rough opening is built up from the constructional hearth and should be large enough to accommodate the fireback and a gap of at least 25mm all around. Table 3.4 gives the recommended dimensions for the rough openings for various fire sizes. It is built with side and back walls at least 200mm thick and 300mm if made from stone. Some designs of fireplace have the hearth raised above floor level. A constructional hearth at or above floor level is still required and the raise must be added to the height of the rough opening. The top of the rough opening will usually be formed by a lintel but a brick arch is a possible alternative. Surrounding masonry must resist the lateral thrust of a brick arch which therefore should not be used across the full width of a breast without a tie rod. Ordinary type iii cement and bricks are used to build the rough opening.

Gather, Throat and Smoke Shelf

The best arrangement is a smooth gather leading to a suitably sized throat followed by a smooth expansion into the flue proper with no sides inclined at more than 45 degrees to the vertical and with no smoke shelf. Specific considerations apply to Rumford type designs because the bottom of the gather is wider than it is deep. If all sides are inclined at the same angle to the vertical, the throat ends up being very wide and narrow. Normally the sides of the gather converge at 45° to the vertical but the front and back converge more gently if at all. The throat constriction is formed front to back as shown in figures 2.6 or 2.7. Such throats are wider than the flue and so a second "gather" is needed to channel the smoke passing through a wide narrow throat into a round or square flue. If a smoke shelf is used the second gather is called a smoke chamber (figure 2.6). This arrangement works OK but a smooth system with no smoke shelf performs better. When tackling a smoking fire with an apparently insurmountable problem like a flue that is too long, convoluted or narrow, such a throat may fix it without having to do extensive chimney rebuilding and is worth a try.

Table 3.4. Rough opening sizes with standard bricks (225×112.5×75mm and a 10mm mortar gap)								
Width		Depth		Height		Largest finished opening allowing a 25mm gap and 76.2mm fireback thickness		
Brick Lengths	mm	Brick Lengths	Mm	Brick Courses	mm	Wide	Deep	Width: Depth
2½	600	1	245	5	435	395	145	2.7
2½	600	1½	360	5	435	395	260	1.5
3	715	1½	360	6	520	510	260	2
3½	830	1½	360	8	690	630	260	2.4
3½	830	2	480	8	690	630	380	1.7
4	950	1½	360	9	775	750	260	2.9
4	950	2	480	9	775	750	380	2
4	950	2½	600	9	775	750	495	1.5
4½	1070	2	480	10	860	865	380	2.3
4½	1070	2½	600	10	860	865	495	1.7
5	1185	2	480	12	1030	980	380	2.6
5	1185	3	715	12	1030	980	615	1.6
6	1420	2½	600	15	1285	1220	495	2.5
6	1420	3	715	15	1285	1220	615	2
7	1655	2½	600	17	1455	1450	495	2.9
7	1655	3	715	17	1455	1450	615	2.4
8	1890	3	715	20	1710	1690	615	1.7
8	1890	4	950	20	1710	1690	850	2
9	2125	3½	830	23	1965	1920	730	2.6
9	2125	4½	1070	23	1965	1920	965	2
Dimensions in mm. To convert to inches divide by 25.4								

Conventional smoke chamber

A smoke shelf is a flat horizontal surface above and behind the throat as shown in figure 3.12. The concept is flawed. It creates

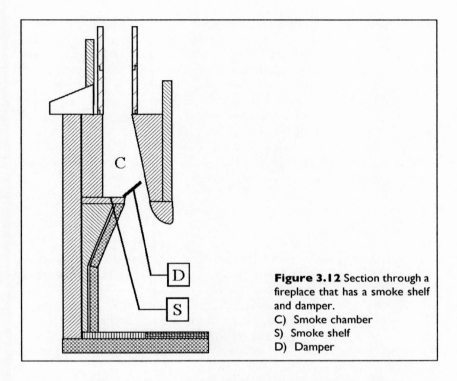

Figure 3.12 Section through a fireplace that has a smoke shelf and damper.
C) Smoke chamber
S) Smoke shelf
D) Damper

turbulence above the throat thereby increasing the overall resistance of the chimney and making it less tolerant of downdrafts. That said these effects have only a minor impact on the fire's functioning. The vast majority of fires both new and old use a smoke shelf and most work perfectly well. There are reasons for using a smoke shelf. One is that you may be reluctant to accept its dismissal when other texts differ. Finding out by trial and error would be expensive and little will be lost by using a smoke shelf.

Another reason for using a smoke shelf is that it simplifies the build if the chimney is built before the fire box. A corbeled smoke chamber is built in the rough opening and may be done before the fireback is put in, in which case the bottom of the chamber is located 10 to 20mm above the height of the top of the throat. The bottom of the chamber is left as an opening. When the throat is installed its top forms the smoke shelf. It may be necessary to allow for a lever to control a damper. When the fire box and throat have been installed the gap between the top of the throat and the bottom of the gather is filled with mortar. This may be possible to do through the throat but check this as with some precast fireboxes it is not and mortar must be laid on around the edge before it is located. Considerable ingenuity is sometimes required to do this. I have in the past cobbled together a nozzle for a pointing gun with a copper pipe bent round 90 degrees and filled the gap through a narrow throat with this, a mirror on a stick and a small inspection lamp. If the breast is left open above the rough opening even with the lintel in place the job is considerably simplified. The problem then is that the front of the smoke chamber (usually the front wall of the breast) must be finished last and the inside of the smoke chamber and throat cleared of any excess mortar via the throat.

Smooth throat

A smooth throat and gather presents more of a challenge to construct. One possible internal shape is shown in figure 2.7. It can be done with precast components or brick. If using brick the internal shape can be made as a plywood former. Bricks can be laid against this with the thinest layer of exposed mortar possible. The plywood former can be removed or burned out later. If burned out it should be left at least 2 weeks because the heat will drive the water out of the mortar and stop it setting. It is a lot easier to build this with the breast incomplete though not impossible without.

Connecting the throat to the first flue liner without a smoke shelf requires some thought. If it is desired to minimise turbulence the inclined surfaces should be smooth rather than corbeled. This can be effected with a cement render but after long use it may fall away landing in the fire or blocking the throat. A better solution is to lay brick so that the gather and throat lining is smooth or to use precast components. Bricks can be laid on a wooden frame which is removed or burned once the mortar has set.

True hearth and fireback

The true hearth and fireback will be in direct contact with the fire. Firebrick and fire cement are used. The mortar gaps between bricks are smaller than normal at about 4mm. Whatever cement is used the fire will eventually erode wide joints so the joints are kept as narrow as possible. Drawings and dimensions are given in figures 3.2-3.9 and tables 3.1-3.3 These dimensions need not be adhered to exactly and can be adjusted to fit the requirements of specific grates or other appliances. They are intended to minimise the amount of brick cutting necessary by making lengths multiples of half firebricks.

The hearth paving can be done with firebricks or fireclay slabs. Firebricks are laid out as stretchers from the center as when tiling a room. They can be laid in conventional Portland cement mortar as in most cases the hearth is separated from the fire by the appliance. Fire cement is used as a grout between the bricks once the concrete or mortar they are laid in has set. It is worked into the joints and scraped flat. The bricks are laid half over each other. If an ash pit is to be used an ash door is installed first and the hearth paving firebricks placed around it. This item has the same dimensions as a firebrick for convenient installation. Once the hearth has been laid the fireback is marked out. The firebricks of the back are usually used in the shiner position (edge horizontal) but this is not essential and if used in the stretcher position (face horizontal) the fireplace will be more durable though cost and space requirements will increase. The firebrick structure should not support the weight of any masonry other than the throat. Consider using soapstone firebricks, if available, for the fireback. Their beauty and performance (see chapter 8) may justify the extra expense.

The corners between the back and sides of the fireback require some consideration. The fireback will be stronger if the bricks of the sides interlock with those of the back but this is likely to require that the ends of bricks are cut with specific angles as large cement gaps will not last. If the fireback is built in an interlocking fashion like this it is more difficult to replace individual bricks later when they crumble. An alternative is to butt join the corners. This leaves triangular spaces behind the corners which are filled by applying fire cement to the ends of the bricks before assembling them. The complexities become even more pronounced with a forward-sloping fireback as there is then no way of avoiding cutting complicated angles in the bricks. Most firebacks of this type employ either precast components or sets of specifically precut firebricks. If a nonstandard forward-sloping fireback design is specified, one solution is to make a wooden mold and cast the fireback out of refractory concrete. The alternative of cutting exact angles in firebricks is certainly possible and gives very attractive results if done accurately. Calculating exact angles in 2 planes is difficult and mistakes in cutting are easy to make wasting expensive firebricks.

Provision for thermal expansion must be made around the outside of the fireback. This can be done by laying corrugated cardboard or mineral wool blanket around the fireback before back filling[†]. If cardboard is used it will later burn out leaving a gap.

Dampers

A damper (throat restrictor) is metal flap that can be moved to adjust the size of the throat while the fire is burning. Several types are available. They are installed over the firebox as shown in figures 3.9, 3.11 and 3.12. Some designs are adjusted by inserting a poker into a ring accessible through the fireplace opening. These are easy to install but inconvenient to adjust. Other types are adjusted with a handle protruding from the fireplace facing. While these require the provision of a suitable gap in the masonry to accommodate the handle, they are preferable in service because the user does not have to get into the area immediately in front of the fire to adjust them. Dampers allow improved efficiency but this effect is much greater in wood burning fires than in coal burning. When the fire is burning the damper is adjusted so that the throat is as narrow as it can be without the fire smoking. Dampers are available off the shelf to suite common designs of fireplace such as the inset type. Dampers for less common types will probably have to be made specially. This should present little problem as they can be simple hinged shutters made of steel plate.

Dampers spoil the smooth gas flow past the throat and induce turbulence. Flue top dampers are available that avoid this problem. They are located near the top of the chimney and control linkages must be run up to them, often as chains within the flue.

Unconventional layouts.

Several designs of fire with more than one face open to the room have become popular. Some of these are shown in figures 3.13-3.16.

Arranging adequate scavenging is always the problem with such designs. If two opposite sides of a fire are open to the room then the same volume normally scavenged around one side must now be scavenged around both, doubling tramp air flow and ventilatory heat losses. This can be compensated for by lowering the lintel to half its

---

† Back filling is filling the space between the rough opening and fireback. A special insulating concrete is usually used (see chapter 8).

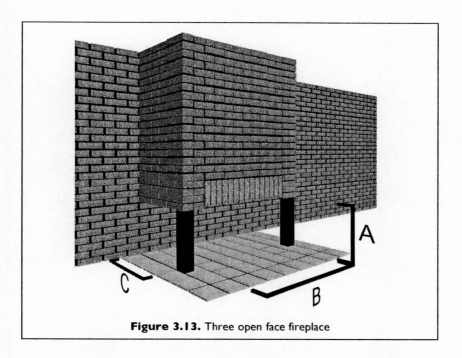

Figure 3.13. Three open face fireplace

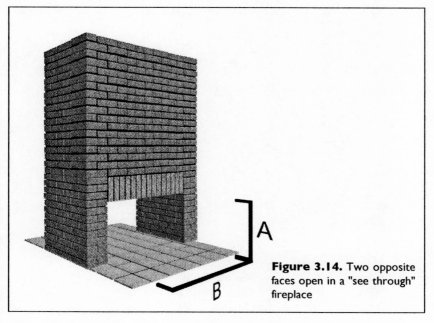

Figure 3.14. Two opposite faces open in a "see through" fireplace

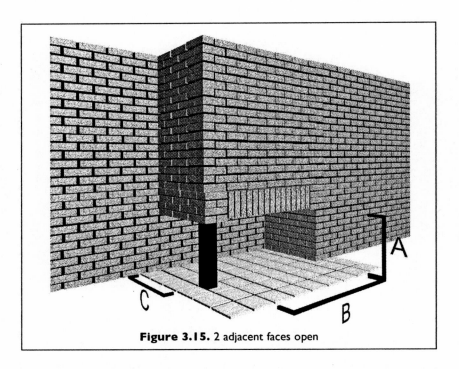

Figure 3.15. 2 adjacent faces open

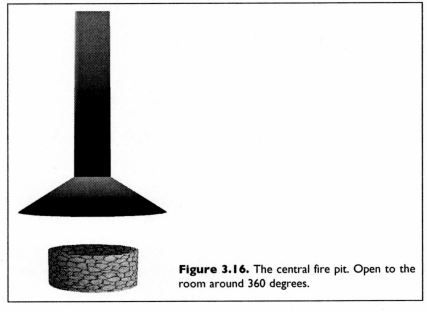

Figure 3.16. The central fire pit. Open to the room around 360 degrees.

corresponding height for an ordinary fire but this to some extent obviates the benefit of having more than one side open as less of the fire can be seen through each open face. A frequently used technique is to raise the fire up on a pedestal to reduce the open area with less lowering of the lintel.

A further complication is that multi-faced fires are susceptible to drafts blowing across the fire from one face to another taking smoke with them. The large tramp air flows involved mean that generous room ventilation is needed and so cross drafts are likely to be a problem. The most extreme types are central fires so beloved of modern architects (figure 3.16). They are among the most decorative and impractical of heating appliances. Even when designed with the greatest care these fires will be prone to smoke and yield little if any useful heat. They can form an attractive feature but take up so much space it is rarely worth it. Chain link curtains are often used to reduce the effect of cross drafts but these impede the view of the fire.

Another frustration with multiple faced fires is that there is little published research on their performance and design optimisation. They are designed by rules of thumb derived from conventional fires. The principle one is the ratio of the fire opening size to that of the flue. For a chimney less than 5m tall the flue cross section area for a multi face fire should be at least 1/8 that of the area of the fire opening. For flues longer than 5m this can be reduced to 1/10 of the opening area. Just what is the area of the fire's opening is not as simple as for an ordinary fire. For a double view fire as shown in figure 3.14 the total opening size is the size of the two openings added together (=$2 \times A \times B$). For a corner fire as shown in figure 3.15 this is too much as the fire acts like a conventional fire facing across the diagonal. The opening size is thus $A\sqrt{B^2 + C^2}$ if B and C are similar. For more complex shapes the effective opening size can be calculated by drawing a circle centered on the grate and tangential to the face nearest to it as shown in figure 3.17 and 3.18.

Reopening old fireplaces.

With the replacement of fireplaces by other means of heating in the middle and late 20th century numerous fireplaces were taken out of use and closed off. The last two decades have seen a resurgence of the popularity of open fires and there has been a consequent demand for

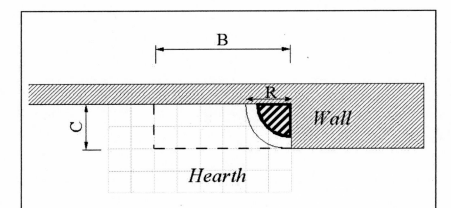

Figure 3.17. Plan of the fireplace shown in figure 3.15 with a corner grate. In this case the height of the lintels (A in figure 3.15) times C + B would be more than the effective open area. A better approximation would be A times the length of the diagonal which is $\sqrt{B^2 + C^2}$. In the situation shown B is a lot longer than C and the best approximation is A times the circumference of a quarter circle with radius R: $A \times \frac{1}{4} \times (2\pi R)$. With this configuration the gather and throat need to be directly above the grate.

reopening of old fireplaces. At its most straightforward this task involves taking down a flimsy partition across the fireplace opening to find an existing grate in which a fire can be built. Needless to say the job is rarely that simple. Most closed fireplaces had long use with little or no maintenance prior to being closed followed by long disuse. Deterioration is to be expected and this particularly affects the chimney lining. There are various recurrent points to note.

Removing pot covers

When a fireplace is taken out of service the chimney top is covered to prevent rain from entering. The commonest way of doing this is to put on a fired clay pot cover. This is a cast clay cover that has small holes to allow some air circulation in the chimney but not large enough to allow smoke egress. Removing pot covers is easy enough as they just lift out but it can be expensive to gain safe access. Health and safety regulations often dictate that scaffolding rather than ladders must be used. Once access to the chimney and pot has been gained, a thorough inspection and repair is recommended to maximise the use of the access.

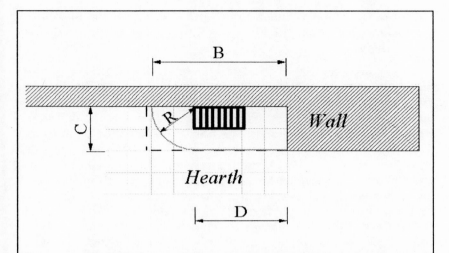

Figure 3.18. Another possible confuguration of the fireplace shown in figure 3.15 this time with the chimney and grate in the middle of the back wall. The height of the lintel (A in figure 3.15) times (C + B) would be a rasonable approximation to the effective open area but better would be A × (('/₄ ×2πR) + D)

Where there is a reasonable looking fireplace

This is the commonest finding when opening an old fireplace. The grate or "appliance" will usually have been removed because most designs protrude forward of the plane of the fireplace face so would have obstructed a flat board covering the opening. Check that the fireback and throat are sound. Cracks and defects can be repaired with fire cement. Chimney testing and repair is covered in chapter 7 but if this passes OK the next thing to do is to find an appliance.

Where there is only a rough opening

Sometimes when a fireplace is reopened only an empty rough opening is found. This may be because there never was a fireback. Houses in the UK built before the 19th century were often like this. Another common cause is that the original fireplace was removed to make way for a stove before eventually being closed up. The biggest problem in this situation is the chimney lining. With luck the lower end of a recognisable lined chimney may be seen. If it is, the fireplace can be built up and attached to it. Provision should be made for the weight of the chimney liners to be born without relying on cement joint adhesion as even if they are solid now, repeated heat cycling may loosen them.

Sometimes the breast is empty to ceiling height. There is often another fireplace in the middle of the breast on the floor above and so the "flue" from the lower fireplace consists of the hollow breast to the ceiling and a narrow passage at the edge of the breast passing the fire on the floor above. It is possible to install a fireplace with a throat that simply opens into the breast cavity and unfortunately many fires are just like this. There is a fair chance of getting away with this in the short term but it cannot be recommended. Such an arrangement is all but impossible to sweep. No brush is large enough to sweep the inside of the breast and finding the entrance to the flue passing the floor above with a brush is difficult, especially if the internal structure is unknown. Draft is liable to be poor because the breast will be filled with turbulent swirling smoke that is cooled on the large surface area. The area of laminar flow at the throat will be short and easily disturbed by downdrafts.

To avoid these problems the fireplace throat must be connected to the flue at ceiling level with a proper lining system. This can be tricky and expensive. Liquid concrete lining (see chapter 7) is a possibility but carries risks. The amount of concrete needed to fill the breast cavity is considerable and the water introduced tends to soak through the masonry taking with it soluble soot products that stain the breast finish – a form of chromatography! Another risk is that a badly decayed breast may bow under the pressure of the liquid concrete. This method is a reasonable option if the finish can easily be restored but not otherwise. The recommended solution is to install liners through the rough opening. In British houses the space inside the breast is usually between 300 and 450mm wide and with a bit of ingenuity it is just about possible for a slim builder to get enough access to do this without tearing down the front wall.

Fire Doors

Glass screens or doors can be fitted in front of a fire to cover the opening and prevent room air from going up the chimney. This radically alters the functioning of a fire. With slower air flow there is less cold air to dilute the high temperature of the smoke and draft pressure increases dramatically. In order for a fire to burn with glass doors closed some venting is necessary within the fire box itself. If this is at low level then a significant amount of direct draft[‡] can occur. This leads to increased air supply to the fire and faster combustion, further increasing draft. Because of these very different burning characteristics glass doors are not usually intended to be closed when the fire is well alight. Their purpose is to improve draft and reduce smoke entry into the room when the chimney is cold and to close the front of the fireplace when the fire is out to prevent warm room air passing up the chimney. Screens are prone to becoming obscured by smoke or being damaged and are not popular in the UK.

[‡] Direct draft is air that is drawn directly through the grate rather than over the top of the fire. The result is a much brisker air supply and more vigorous fire. Stoves use direct draft. On a larger scale the heat of solid fuel fired furnaces and pottery kilns illustrate the potential of direct draft.

Chapter 4
Appliances

In the context of fireplaces the term "appliance" refers to the metal bit that holds the fuel while it burns. The term is broad and includes the various types of grate, andirons, stoves or indeed central heating boilers or cooking stoves.

Appliances are broadly divisible into stoves and open fires. Stoves are considerably more energy efficient but lack the aesthetics of an open fire and heating can be achieved even more cheaply and conveniently with gas or oil fired systems where these are available. The market for solid fuel stoves is thus quite specialised. The aesthetic appeal of an open fire is the usual reason why one is installed so open fires and stoves are not really in the same market.

Certain appliances are said to be "approved" by the British Domestic Solid Fuel Approval Scheme. The list of approved appliances, which is published annually, is not binding and is by no means exhaustive. It does not include appliances that exclusively burn wood or many of foreign origin. Even so the standards of safety and efficiency required for approval are among the toughest in the world so an appliance that has been approved is a good one but no approval does not make it poor.

There are 5 broad categories of open fireplace appliance on the market today: those where the complete fireplace including the fireback, gather and throat are designed as a unit, controllable grates, partially controllable grates, baskets and andirons.

Complete fireplace

Numerically, complete fireplace assemblies are the market leaders if living flame gas fires are included. Such gas fires are a very good choice of appliance particularly in areas where smoke control legislation is in effect. They are discussed in more detail in chapter 6. They come with complete fitting instructions that require little skill or knowledge of the design and building of fireplaces.

There are several solid fuel burning complete fireplace assemblies available and as with living flame gas fires their installation does not demand any particular specialist knowledge. All that is required is a suitably size rough opening and a class 1 flue to connect them to.

There is a difficulty with many of these products in that too much emphasis, both in design and in marketing, is placed on improving their thermal efficiency. This involves compromise of fire visibility, smoke free operation, and quite often ease of igniting and burning as well. They are typically relatively low, deep fire boxes made from cast-iron or fabricated steel sheet. They will often include a damper and throat. They may have doors which can be closed or left open with the fire burning. Those with doors are designed for more direct draft than open fires. They frequently perform poorly with the doors open having a tendency to go out or smoke. If a heating appliance is wanted then a gas fire or central heating system will be found to be the most competitive products on the market. If an open fire is wanted for its aesthetics there can be little justification for compromising this in exchange for improvement in a secondary function at which it performs poorly at best. For these reasons manufactured complete fireplaces must be considered with great care to ensure that what is purchased is actually what is wanted.

These comments do not extend to prefabricated concrete or cut stone firebacks or complete fire boxes including back, gather and throat as these are really a refinement of conventional fire construction and some of the finest fireplaces available are made in this way.

Controllable grate

A controllable grate uses sliding doors or shutters under the fire to control the amount of air passing through it and so control the burn rate. Such grates have to be sealed into the fireplace with fire cement in order to prevent excess air getting into the fire around the sides rather than through the control vents. They are generally not as attractive as other types of appliance but have the advantage that the fire can be made to burn very slowly even with large amounts of fuel heaped on. This type of grate is a good choice when it is desirable for the fire to burn for long period of time without being replenished with fuel. The practical limit is about 10 hours for coal fires. Because controllable grates have to be sealed into the bottom of the fireplace they have to be a fairly tight fit. They are available to fit standard fireplace sizes, most in the UK being for 400mm or 450mm "inset" fires. Controllable grates are not generally available for non standard fireplace sizes such as those found in the drawings and tables of chapter 3.

Semi-controllable grates

Semi controllable grates are generally less expensive than fully controllable ones. They have a metal plate at the front below the grate with often not very effective slats that can be opened or closed allowing some degree of control. These grates are not fire cement sealed and the degree of control afforded is rather limited. They do not allow burn rates low enough for a fire to stay alight unattended for several hours. In practice they operate rather as baskets except they are made to fit into fires where a simple basket design is not suitable because of the shape of the hearth. As with controllable grates they are made to fit standard fireplace designs like the British inset range but the accuracy of the fit is less critical.

Basket

A fire basket is a rectangular structure which is simply a metal basket with no facility to control airflow at all. There may not even be an ash pan. They are generally used in rectangular rough opening fires without a fireback (chapter 3) where they often do not occupy the complete area of the hearth as shown in figure 6.4. Many designs are available with a cast iron fireback.

When using a basket and fireback arrangement it is not necessary to line the fire box with firebricks because flames rarely if ever come into contact with the brick.

Baskets can hold a lot of fuel and can produce a tremendous amount of heat when fully loaded especially if they contain coal. The disadvantage is that the only means of controlling the burn rate is controlling the rate at which fuel is added. They are usually used with wood and to keep a reasonable fire burning logs have to be added every 10 to 20 minutes. This rather limits their application to areas where people are available to do this. Baskets are among the most attractive appliances often displaying considerable artistry which can make them expensive.

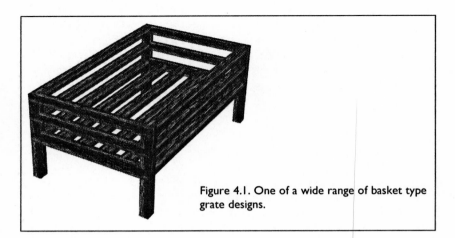

Figure 4.1. One of a wide range of basket type grate designs.

Andirons

Most fires before the 17th century in England used andirons* rather than a grate. They are suitable for burning wood but not coal so they fell out of use as coal burning took over from wood. They are now rarely used in Britain but should not be dismissed. They make for a particularly attractive fire that is easy to light but like a basket allow no control over the burn rate beyond that determined by the rate at which logs are added.

Andirons burn longer logs than grates so less wood cutting is needed. Once the fire is well alight they can burn thicker logs than is feasible in most grates so reducing the need for splitting as well. The andiron "heads" that project up in at the front of the fire remain comparatively free from soot so that when cool they can be picked up and removed from the hearth to allow easy sweeping.

Several designs are available thanks to their continued popularity in wood burning areas such as North America.

Many andirons have decorative brass uprights but it is quite possible for a wood fire to get hot enough to melt brass so the backs of andirons should be made of iron!

When andirons are used, logs are cut into lengths of 450 to 900mm depending on the distance between the andiron backs. The logs are stacked on the andirons and the fire kindled in the space under

---

*. Andirons also go by the name of "fire dogs" from their obvious resemblance to dogs.

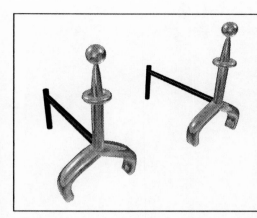

Figure 4.2. A pair of andirons. The "back" of the andirons here shown coloured black should be able to withstand high temperatures so should be made of a ferrous metal. The decorative fronts are often made from brass.

them in the middle of the hearth. As the logs pass into the third phase of combustion (charcoal - see chapter 9) they break and sag in the middle with the ends still supported on the andirons. The charcoal is left to burn on the hearth and further logs stacked above it. The outer ends of the logs are periodically moved back between the andirons once they have fallen.

Inevitably personal preferences vary but my ideal fireplace is a Rumford design built out of soapstone and using andirons rather than a grate.

Inset fires

The term "inset" fires refers to a standard range of fireplace fittings used in Britain. They are conventional fires designed primarily to burn coal, and so are considerably smaller than their North American cousins which mainly burn wood. They are built around pre-moulded fireclay firebacks which are available in widths from 300mm to 600mm in steps of 50mm. The 400mm is the most common (figure 4.3) followed by the 450mm. Standard components such as firebacks and lintels are available in these two sizes from most builders merchants.

More specialised suppliers will be required for the other sizes and it is likely to be easier to build a firebrick back than to source the rarer sizes these days.

A range of parts is available to fit the standard dimensions of these designs including grates of various degrees of sophistication, dampers, ash pans and pits, gathers, lintels and throats. Inset appliances are of the controllable or semi controllable type. The controllable ones have

Figure 4.3. A 400mm inset fire fitted with a controllable grate and overnight burning plate (hinged down just below the bars). This one has a serious smoking problem evidenced by the black stain above the lintel.

an option of deepening bars or overnight burning plates, allowing more coal to be loaded and extended burning times of up to 10 hours.

Back boilers, sometimes known as boiler flue sets, are available for inset fires. They come in two power outputs. Standard back boilers give about 3kW to the water and high output types give 6.6kW.

The power output of these is small by comparison with modern central heating appliances and they are now rarely used but do find a niche in such settings as holiday cottages away from gas mains and as supplementary heating where wood fuel is available free. They are made of cast iron or fabricated steel. For radiators they should be connected via an indirect heat exchange cylinder that includes a pressure release safety valve. They require descaling in hard water areas and access is provided for this. Some are glass lined to prevent corrosion when used in soft water areas.

Holes in the wall

Fires can be lifted off the floor in which case the constructional hearth can be built at floor level or raised to the level of the fire. The main limitation of this design is the tendency for burning objects to fall out of the fire especially if it is a shallow one. This means that the best designs of solid fuel fires are not suitable for deployment as a hole-in-the-wall. The safety, clean burning and convenience of gas fires makes them much more suited to this type of design. Hole-in-the-wall fires go particularly well with modern architectural styles and the overall effect is at its best with the more artistic contemporary gas fires shown in chapter 6.

Fan assisted fires

These are not to be confused with chimney fans. It is possible to buy fan assisted installations for certain open fires. These fans blow air through the fire. This acts like a turbo charger in an internal combustion engine. Fuel will burn more quickly increasing heat output. These are not likely to be chosen as primary installations but may be used if an existing open fire is the only source of heating but has inadequate power. A limitation is that the flue requirements are increased to those of a physically larger fire by the addition of a fan which may make a fire smoke if the chimney draft was marginal without it.

Convector fires

A number of fireplace designs are available that extract some of the heat from the rising smoke and surrounding masonry and return it to the room thus improving efficiency. The disadvantage is that as the smoke is cooler there will be less draft which may be inadequate in an otherwise marginal situation. The basic design of convector fires is a firebox in a metal jacket around which air can circulate. This air is heated and passed into the same room as the fire or even distributed around the house in more elaborate systems. Some convector type fires are available as free standing units which do not require a breast.

Convector fires are limited in how much heat they can extract from the smoke by the need to keep draft and tramp air flow high enough to prevent smoke from entering the room. For this reason if flames are to be viewed directly inside a building then whatever the fireplace it will be inefficient compared to other systems. Complexities aimed at improving their efficiency do not alter this basic fact and are rarely justifiable. The only thing that can be done to a fireplace to make it efficient is to put doors on it – in other words turn it into a stove.

Chapter 5
Masonry Heaters

Masonry heaters are solid fuel fired storage heaters. They consist of a stove type fireplace with doors which are closed once the fire is alight and a large mass of masonry through which the flue passes via a convoluted course. This comprises a system of baffles and chambers beyond which is a conventional chimney. The masonry surrounding this winding flue is heated by the hot flue gases from a fire that is burned once or twice per day. After the fire has gone out the mass of brickwork remains hot and heats the room for several hours. Masonry heaters are normally constructed entirely within a building and not against an outside wall to minimize heat losses.

Masonry heaters are specifically suited to certain geographical areas. They were developed to provide domestic heating in areas with cold climates and wood as the principle fuel. These are circumstances where open fireplaces perform particularly badly, as described in chapter 2. Because of their poor and frequently negative efficiency alternatives were sort. Masonry heaters reduce by 5 times or more the amount of wood required to heat a house and need far less attention as they are fired only once or twice per day. They were developed in northern and eastern Europe where they have been in use for centuries. They are now becoming popular in North America where they are often referred to according to their country of origin i.e. Finnish, Russian, Swedish, German or Austrian fireplaces or stoves. In the UK where winters are mild and coal is still widely available there has never been the impetus to develop their use. Almost all designs of masonry heater available are intended for wood burning. There is no reason why successful coal burning masonry heaters cannot be built and many wood-fired types can burn coal though the charge will be smaller. In general other means of coal fired heating, such as iron stoves, will be equally or more competitive in areas where coal is readily available.

Thermal efficiency is the main advantage that masonry heaters have over open fireplaces. They can achieve 70 to 80% thermal efficiency which is better than can realistically be achieved with virtually all other types of stove under most conditions and a vast improvement over that of open fires under any conditions.

A second advantage is that they are clean, burning wood or coal more thoroughly and thus giving off less smoke or particulate emissions than open fires. This is because the fire burns quickly with an abundant air supply. The usual way of regulating the rate at which a fire burns is to restrict the air supply but this makes the fire burn with incomplete combustion and a lot of smoke. With a masonry heater the object is to burn a brisk complete fire with abundant air and then for it to go out so this problem is avoided. The particulate emission figures for masonry heaters are similar to those of the cleanest solid fuel burning stoves but in practice masonry heaters do even better because such stoves use a system of secondary combustion of smoke which does not work well at heat settings below about 2kW. No such problems apply to Masonry heaters because if low heat outputs are required smaller fires are burned less frequently. In the USA Masonry heaters are commonly permitted in smoke control areas. With their high efficiency, clean burning and use of renewable fuel (wood), masonry heaters are unrivaled from an environmental point of view!

They are not without their disadvantages. They are large installations, typically occupying a cubic meter or more. They are built entirely inside the house and cannot be moved once installed. In their simple form they are rather uncontrollable. They take some time to heat up and cannot be turned on and off at will. Unless you DIY, they are expensive and in the UK it is difficult to find builders with the necessary knowledge to build one properly. Many of these problems have been addressed in northern Europe and the US with increasingly sophisticated designs. Several prefabricated models are available greatly simplifying construction and often allowing additional features such as controllability, water heating or integral cooking ovens. Such ovens are always hot while the heater is in use and have very stable temperature which, I am told, allows for superior cooking!

As is explained in chapter 2, open fires have very marginal draft performance requiring wide, straight, warm chimneys to prevent smoking. Eefficiency is maximized if tramp air is eliminated and aniway a glance at figure 5.1 shows that the flue path of a masonry heater is totally incompatible with an open fire. For these reasons masonry heaters have direct draft and stove doors which were traditionally made of cast iron. Increasing demand for the decorative aesthetics of open fires has brought some design improvements. Glazed stove doors are available and many designs of masonry heater incorporate a system of movable baffles which can be switched to convey the smoke through the heater in the usual way or divert it directly to the chimney to make lighting easier and allowing the heater to be used as a fire with the doors open. When the baffle is turned to bypass the heater it is arranged that the air flow through the heater is completely blocked to prevent convective cooling.

Design

The parameters which largely determine the design of the heater are the required heat output and the frequency of firing. These determine how much heat has to be stored. The standard size of bricks used in the UK is 225×112.5×75mm. If a 10mm mortar joint is included around 4 sides this becomes 235×112.5×85mm (in a wall, ignoring edge effects, there are 2 mortar joints per brick). Brick and mortar masonry has a volumetric heat capacity given in table 11.1 of around 1950J/l°C. This gives a wall built with solid bricks a heat capacity of about 4.4kJ/°C per brick.

To calculate the required heat storage capacity it is necessary to know the heating power required and the time between firings. For a single room this may be around 4kW and if the firing frequency is 8 hourly the heater must supply 4000J/s for 8 hours so must store about 115MJ. In principle the temperature of the bricks inside the heater could be made very high but that would mean wide fluctuation in heat output as the heater would cool so much between firings. From this point of view the cooler the better. In practice a core temperature below 500°C is used and a typical range for a firing and cooling cycle is from 350° to 100°C. This range gives a heat capacity per brick of 250×4400J or 1.1MJ. The heater must therefore contain 115000000/1100000 = 105 bricks. A complication is that the whole outer wall of a masonry heater does not all reach the core temperature, the outer surface remaining cooler than the inner. Heaters can be built with single or double brick outer walls. In the case of double wall heaters a 25mm insulating layer or air gap is left between the wythes of the wall and the heat capacity can reasonably be reckoned by counting only the bricks of the inner wall. With a single wall heater a reasonable approximation is to halve the number of bricks in the wall to reckon heat capacity. A practical heater would be around 30-50% flue passages so the overall volume would be around 400 litres. That is about 2000×500×400mm, i.e. a rather small chimney breast.

In North America a single masonry heater may be used to heat an entire house with firing only once per day. In this case the total maximum heat output in the winter might average 20kW with up to 30 during the day and less at night. This demands a heat storage capacity of 20000J/s for 24 hours or 1.7GJ. Using the values given above the heater would need to contain about 1500 bricks and have a volume of around 550ol. Such a heater would typically be constructed in the center of the house and consist of a column of around 4m high (over 2 floors) by 1.2 by 1.2m.

Internal structure

The internal design of a masonry heater is a system of brick walls with gaps that directs flue gases around them. The exact way in which this is achieved is not that important as long as certain factors are borne in mind. Successful designs vary from tall columns with the flue going up and down to long low structure like benches with the flue going back and forth. Figures 5.1 and 5.2 show examples. The design of masonry heaters is complicated by the need to accommodate thermal

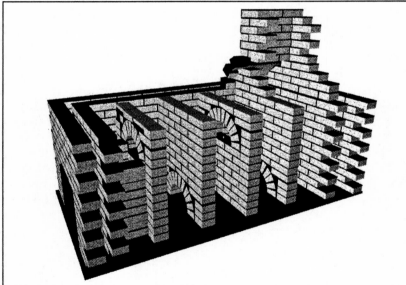

Figure 5.1. Cut away view of a masonry heater with 4 vertical chambers and 2 wythe walls. For clarity the baffles have been drawn widely separated. A practical heater would be shorter or contain an extra chamber.

Figure 5.2. A smaller masonry heater built within a chimney breast shown without the front wall. This design uses one wythe walls. The flue path is up the central section down on the right, under the fire and up to the chimney on the left. Flue liners are used to channel the flue gases under the fire which is located on the black slab.

cycling. In terms of furnace construction the temperatures reached by masonry heaters, even in the fire box, are modest but the repeated heating and cooling leads to expansion and contraction which will rapidly lead to the structure crumbling if thermal cycling is not allowed for. Furthermore it is guaranteed that the surface rendering or tiling of the heater will crack within a few weeks of use if the expansion of the core is not isolated from the surface. The coefficients of thermal expansion of brick, concrete and steel are $5\text{-}7\times10^{-6}$, $7\text{-}14\times10^{-6}$, and $10\text{-}18\times10^{-6}$ /°C meaning that with a 350°C temperature range 1m of each will expand 2, 3-5, and 3-6mm respectively.

It is not economic or practical to allow completely for thermal cycling. During a firing the brick surfaces adjacent to the fire heat up rapidly while the rear surfaces of the bricks remain cooler leading to differential expansion between the inner and outer surfaces and internal stresses in the bricks.

Similarly stresses are inevitable between adjacent bricks of differing temperature and it is not necessary to allow expansion joints between each brick as a certain amount of thermal stress can be tolerated by bricks and mortar.

The first principle of thermal stress accommodation is therefore not to eliminate but to minimize it. A simple but effective way of doing this is to design the heater with two parts, both of which have fairly uniform temperatures, one being the hot core and the other the cool surface. These parts are separated by a flexible insulating junction.

Even when this is done with great care it is probable that some thermal cracking will occur over prolonged use. If the most carefully designed and built heater is dismantled after 50 years of regular use it is unlikely that no thermal cracking will be found. The second principle of thermal stress accommodation is therefore to make the structure tolerant of such cracking. The gaps in the baffles are prone to becoming blocked if thermal stress leads to disintegration of the masonry. Figure 5.3 shows different ways of building the baffles. The arch in figure 5.3c is the most durable solution as all stresses on the brick are compressive. The gap in figure 5.3b is satisfactory only if a steel strip is included as shown though such strips don't last for ever. Without it the bricks above the gap are sure to fall into it when the adhesion of the mortar fails, which it will. The corbeled arch of figure 5.3a is poor. It will withstand failure of mortar adhesion but heat cycling is liable to make bricks crack through the middle. This, coupled with mortar failure, will result in half bricks falling into the gap.

Load bearing thermal expansion joints are considerably more complex than non load bearing especially if they have to be refractory. Fortunately the temperature rise in a heater at the bottom is modest and such stresses that do arise can be distributed over several courses of brick so the bottom of both the hot core and outer wall of the heater can be built directly onto the constructional hearth.

The height of the heater including the fireplace and baffle system but excluding the chimney should not exceed about 5m. For large heaters the outer wall is best made of 2 brick wythes with a 25mm cavity. This arrangement prevents any cracks in the inner layer propagating through the outer wythe and causing the heater to leak. Also the heater relies on releasing heat slowly to the room so insulation is advantageous within the brick wall. If no air gap is used the heater will run hotter after a firing and cool more quickly. In small heaters the space occupied by 2 wythe walls is not justified (figure 5.2) and 1 wythe

Figure 5.3. Three different ways of building the gaps in baffles.

A is a poor solution because thermal cycling is likely to lead to failure of mortar adhesion as well as bricks cracking through the middle. Half bricks could fall and block the gap.

B shows a steel strip used to support the overlying brick work. It is better than A but the steel will not last for ever and when it fails obstruction is likely.

C is the best solution. All loads on the arch are compressive and it will not collapse when the mortar adhesion fails.

walls can be used but the baffles should still be isolated from the outer walls. Baffles can be of pre-cast concrete, concrete cast in situ or single wythe brick work. They will expand with heat and a gap of 10-20mm should be left between the baffles and the walls. This gap can later be filled with a refractory packing like mineral wool. The cross sectional area of the path defined by the baffles should be between 400 and

1000cm². At no point should this area be less than 400cm². No more than 5 baffle chambers are recommended. The design of the fireplace will be dictated by the fire door and grate system chosen. The firebox should be lined with firebrick and fire cement or formed of fire clay or soap stone components. This refractory lining should extend to the top of the first baffle or 1m above the grate. Above this the baffle system can be vertical or horizontal. Building regulations require that the entire heater is built on a conventional constructional hearth that extends 500mm in front of and 150mm either side of the fire doors.

The top - sometimes called the crown - presents a problem in a large heater because it cannot be built as a cavity wall. One solution is to use a thick brick layer - 300mm or so. This spreads the temperature gradient and reduces thermal stresses and conductivity. Designs with concrete slabs and insulating layers are also possible.

The exact path of the flue gases is not critical. The design in figure 5.2 uses 230mm flue liners to make the path along the bottom. This idea can be extended for long low designs which may employ lengths of flue liner going back and forth. The heat stored in the masonry will be in the baffles and inner walls so they should be made of solid rather than perforated bricks.

An oven can be built into the inner masonry accessible via a door in the outer brickwork. Ingenuity with variable ventilation of the oven can even allow a degree of temperature control.

The conventional design allows no control over the rate at which heat is given to the room. Controllability can be allowed by, for example, incorporating ducts made from 125mm chimney liners placed upside down running through the hot block and connected to a gated convection system.

Materials

Where double wythe walls are used the outer wythe will be exposed to modest temperatures and no corrosive smoke and gases and so can be built with conventional brick and type iii mortar. The inner wythe and baffle system must withstand these rigors but does not have to be particularly strong. Type iv mortar is preferable but type iii can be used (see chapter 8). Solid brick should be used for most of the structure and firebrick with fire cement for the fire box and the first 1m of the flue path or until the first turn into the baffle system. Masonry heaters burn fuel efficiently and need infrequent cleaning but provision should be made for this. At points such as access points for cleaning and oven doors if an oven is installed consideration must be given to thermal expansion and heat conduction. Various schemes will work but simply squaring off the edge of the wall with brick mortared to the inner and outer wythe is not recommended. Metal clear out or oven door frames that are deep enough to traverse both wythes can be used and fixed rigidly to the outer wythe only allowing some movement to occur between the frame and inner wythe.

Grates are generally made of ferrous metal and are comparable in size to generous fireplace grates, 300 by 300mm being typical for a medium sized heater.

Chapter 6

Gas Fires

T he UK market for open fires has expanded considerably in the last 15 years thanks to the popularity of modern gas burning fireplaces. They offer greater economy and convenience than their solid fuel burning counterparts but the principal reason for the change is the extent of smoke control areas. Most of the population of the UK now lives in such areas. The only alternative to gas burning open fires in these areas is to use smokeless fuel in regular fireplaces but this is expensive and the appearance is remarkably similar to that of a gas fire and in some ways is inferior in that a flickering yellow flame effect can be achieved with a gas fire but not with smokeless fuel.

Modern gas fires can be divided into three types: radiant fires, living flame fires, and decorative flame effect (DFE) fires. The most efficient but least attractive of these are radiant fires. Living flame fires have reasonable heat output and decorative appeal. DFE fires are not really intended as practical heating appliances but rather as decorations. Their useful heat output is very variable as they are prone to all the uncertainties of solid fuel open fires and they rarely yield more than 2kW. Any fire where the flames can be seen must have some tramp air flow even if small as in the case of radiant gas fires and this means a drawing flue, either of natural draft or fan drawn type.

Radiant Fires

The term "radiant fire" refers to the familiar gas fire design with a ceramic radiating surface that is heated by gas flames (figure 6.1). The market for this type of gas fire has declined in recent years as they have been squeezed between the economy and convenience of gas fired central heating systems on one hand and the better aesthetics of modern living flame gas fires on the other. Nevertheless they are still available and the performance of modern models is exceptionally good. Heat power output is typically in the range from 4 to 6kW with thermal

Figure 6.1. A radiant gas fire, this model dating from the 1970s.

efficiencies of 75% percent or so. They are a good choice of appliance in environments were central heating is not available and efficient clean and safe heating is required but appearance is not the primary concern. Certain styles of contemporary interior decor, particularly those employing steel, glass, and clean uncluttered lines may be better suited to this kind of fire than the more popular living flame type.

Living Flame Fires

The term "living flame" refers to fires that use flickering gas flames and ceramic "coals" to simulate solid fuel fires. Initially when this type of fire was introduced the term was used to distinguish them from radiant gas fires. It is now used to refer to a specific type of living flame gas fire that is designed for both aesthetic appeal and reasonable thermal efficiency (figure 6.2). When first introduced in the 1970s the system was not that good with low efficiency, poor aesthetics, and a tendency to look shabby after a short time interval. Great improvements have been made and modern examples are convenient, reliable, and remarkably life like, so much so that people often throw paper on to them unaware that they are not real fires. The system employs gas flames trained onto a collection of refractory ceramic fibre (RCF) lumps. RCF is a silicate-aluminate ceramic material which can be formed as an open network of randomly oriented fibres with a very low overall density and hence volumetric heat capacity meaning that they heat up very quickly. RCF is also an extremely poor conductor of heat so one side of a "coal" can be glowing red hot while the other is

Figure 6.2. Living flame gas fire. An attractive, tolerably efficient and cost effective choice.

cool enough to touch. This combination of properties not only gives a very realistic visual effect but also makes living flame fires safe as even touching a red hot coal is unlikely to cause a serious burn. RCF lumps are usually shaped and coloured to look like coals but they can be made in almost any shape and colour and a wide range of shapes such as pebbles and geometric forms are available for use in contemporary designs.

Figure 6.3. An inset insert gas fire. Not as efficient as a living flame fire but attractive and very cost effective if an inset fireplace already exists. This fireback has cracked from heat cycling when used with a coal fire before the gas insert was installed.

Living flame fires are usually supplied as complete installations which include the gas burner, RCF coals, fireback and throat formation and connect directly onto the bottom of the flue. Comprehensive fitting instructions come with the appliances and there is little need for any detailed knowledge of fireplace design or construction on the part of the fitter.

The performance of living flame fires is reasonable with useful heat output into the room ranging from 3 to 4½ kW. Thermal efficiency is typically 40%, a considerable improvement on most open fires but not as good as radiant gas fires.

A common and inexpensive variant on living flame fires is the "inset insert" fire. This consists of a gas burner, grate and RCF coals only and is designed to fit directly into a 400 or 450mm standard UK inset fireplace. In this case the installer must only plumb gas to the appliance as it is designed to work with the flue system of the standard open fire. The performance of these inset insert fires is not as good as that of a true living flame fire with efficiency in the 20-35% region but purchase and installation costs are much lower if an inset fireplace is already present.

Decorative Flame Effect Fires

Decorative Flame (or Fuel) Effect (DFE) fires are designed primarily as decorations with only secondary consideration being given to thermal efficiency. Consequently their thermal efficiency is poor with useful heat outputs typically not more than 2 kW and efficiency figures below 25%. As decorations they are the best options available in smoke control areas and consequently they are very popular (figure

Figure 6.4. A DFE gas fire. This model has a cast iron fireback but it does not act as an effective radiant surface. The fireplace is a rough opening with no firebrick fireback.

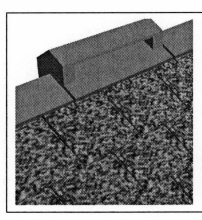

Figure 6.5. Example of the type of top used on a precast flue. They are made form fired clay or cast concrete and come in various forms, this one for a roof crest.

6.4). They are usually supplied in 2 parts. These are a solid fuel grate designed to burn coal or wood and a standard gas burning insert made to fit within it. This system means that a very wide variety of grates is available ranging from contemporary to period designs. A cast-iron fireback is an option with some designs but the fireplace opening, masonry fireplace, gather, throat and flue system must be built separately - unlike with living flame fires. This should present no major problem because quite often when a DFE design is being considered it will be installed in an existing fireplace. If a new fireplace is being built or an existing one significantly altered the design requirements are as for open fires generally. DFE fires do produce small amounts of soot so annual chimney sweeping is recommended when they are in use.

Chimneys

Building regulation requirements for chimneys are simple for solid fuel burning appliances as the same rules apply to all types. In the UK suitable chimney flues are known as a "class 1". The clean burning and predictability of gas fires has enabled designs to be developed that are far less stringent in their flue requirements. This has resulted in a variety of flue options. Houses built before the demise of solid fuel heating generally have class 1 flues but those built since, if they have chimneys at all, may have one of several designs.

Frequently the main determinant of what kind of fire can be installed is what type of flue is in the room to begin with as substantial changes to the flue installation are likely to be considerably more expensive than the fireplace installation itself. The types of flue for which gas fires are available range from no flue at all to conventional class 1 chimneys. In most cases it is easy to tell which kind of flue, if any, is present by looking at the chimney top. A terracotta or concrete vent on the roof crest as in figure 6.5 is found with a precast flu. A protruding metal chimney with a grill as in figure 6.7 is found on a class 2 flue. This sometimes has a rotating spherical grill. A conventional stack and chimney pot as in figure 6.8 means a class 1 flue.

Figure 6.6. Precast concrete block with a cavity. Cavities are designed to line up when the blocks are laid half over each other to form a "precast" flue.

Figure 6.7. Top of a prefabricated "class 2" flue system.

No Flue

Flueless gas fires use catalytic converters similar to those employed in motor cars to oxidise the small amount of carbon monoxide produced to carbon dioxide so that the fumes from the fire contain virtually nothing but water and carbon dioxide. As these are non-toxic they can be discharged directly into the room. With no flue there is no pathway for heat to be lost from the appliance other than into the room so thermal efficiency is 100%. Adequate ventilation must still be provided in the room to supply oxygen and remove the carbon dioxide and water vapour produced. Partly to limit carbon dioxide and water production and partly because the 100% efficiency eliminates the need to allow for differing heat outputs, flueless gas fires have limited heat outputs of 1.5 to 3kW. They are the most economic heating appliances of all including modern condensing gas boilers! The catalytic converters they contained make them expensive but installation is very straightforward as nothing more than suitable sighting and a gas pipe is required. Several designs are available that are made to look like open fires or contemporary features. They must be enclosed and so if the flame is visible it is behind glass.

Balanced Flue

A balanced flue employs two vents on an outside wall, one of which serves to draw air into the appliance for combustion and the other to discharge flue gases. The two vents may be combined within the same cowl structure and some systems use coaxial or side by side

Figure 6.8. Chimney tops of this type with terracotta pots denote a class I flue.

two channel flue pipes. The system is enclosed and separated from the room air and thus any visible fire must be behind glass as with the flueless system. Unlike the flueless system no room oxygen is used and no carbon dioxide or water is discharged into the room. Some loss of heat via the flue gas occurs and efficiencies are in the region of 70-80%. Both radiant and living flame fires are available in balanced flue configuration. The big advantage of the system is that a natural draft flue is not necessary and thus there need be no vertical components to the chimney. Is not even necessary for the appliance to be on an outside wall as the flue pathway can be about 2m long in a horizontal direction.

Class 2 Flue

The term "class 2 flue" refers to a range of natural draft flue designs which are not suitable for solid fuel burning but can be used for gas fires. Some confusion exists about the term. It originates from British building regulation where it refers to flues that comply with BS5440 part 1 and 2. This includes twin wall prefabricated flues complying with BS715 or equivalent and having a minimum diameter of 125mm and a minimum height of 3m – commonly known as "class 2" flues. It also includes pre-fabricated flue block systems complying with BS1289. Although strictly also class 2 these are commonly known as "precast" flues. They are formed from special concrete blocks with outside dimensions to fit in with other masonry units used to build internal walls but containing cavities that together form a channel (figure 6.6.).

The range of appliances that can use these two types differs slightly hence the distinction in common parlance of "class 2" or "precast".

DFE fires require a class 1 flue but other types of gas fire are generally available in variants that can use class 2 or precast flues.

Fan Drawn Flue.

With solid fuel open fires a chimney fan is usually regarded as a remedial measure for a poorly drawing chimney but it is quite popular as a primary design where gas fires are being considered. The flue gases coming from gas fires are far more benign than those coming from solid fuel fires so chimney fans can be considerably less robust and expensive. Most types of gas fire can be installed with a fan drawn flue including some decorative flame effect designs though careful matching of fan to fireplace may be necessary. Longer and more convoluted flue pathways are possible than would otherwise be the case. The disadvantages are a small penalty in electric power consumption and of course reliability.

Figure 6.9 decorative flame effect fire by Verine. Picture courtesy of Verine Ltd, UK.

Figure 6.10 "Dancing flames" by Verine.

A fan drawn flue is the only way of allowing direct viewing of flames (i.e. not behind glass) without having a chimney and natural draft flue. Because of this several gas fire installations are available that are configured for or include a flue fan which may be at the fireplace end or on the outside wall.

Class 1 Flue

A class 1 flue is a natural draft flue as used for solid fuel fires. The British building regulations require that it has a minimum diameter of 175mm and be lined with an appropriate material. The constraints on gas fire flues are less stringent. Radiant, living flame and DFE fires can all be used with this type of flue but only DFE fires must have a class 1 or fan drawn flue. The draft requirement of gas fires is in general lower than of solid fuel burning fires and a class 1 flue may draw too much. For this reason a draft regulator is often fitted when a gas fire is used with a class 1 flue. This is a device that allows additional cool air to be drawn into the flue at a point above the throat without the flue gases escaping.

Contemporary design with gas fires

The flexibility and clean burning of gas has allowed the development of a wide range of designs which are not subject to the

Figure 6.11 Olympic 70 design by Verine. The appliance shown makes a good choice for a modern hole in the wall fire.

constraints that limit solid fuel fires. This has led to the creative use of flame as an item of decoration. Modern designs that depart from the traditional fireplace appearance fall into two categories. Firstly there are those that use the principle of a ceramic surface heated by a flame which radiates heat into the room. These are of the living flame type with the distinction that the RCF lumps are not made to look like coal but rather made to be decorative items in their own right. The technical performance of such fires is as for conventional living flame fires.

It is in the second type where the creative use of flame reaches its pinnacle. Fires of this type focus on the flames themselves rather than heated RCF lumps. They are similar to decorative flame effect fires in that they are designed primarily for appearance rather than efficiency. Figures 6.9 – 6.11 show examples.

Chapter 7
Chimneys

Introduction

Chimneys are troublesome. They let in rain, they are dirty, and when the fire is not lit they provoke cold drafts. If not swept regularly they are prone to chimney fires or soot falls covering what is usually the best room with an indelible oily black coating, and that is when they are working properly. Frequently they are not. They rot, especially at the top. This leads to leakage of smoke filling usually the attic and hence upper story. In terraces the smoke can track along the roof space and enter adjacent houses. As the mortar is eaten away from the stack it becomes unsafe, waiting for a high wind to blow a ton of masonry down through the roof, the ceiling, and whatever lies below. The divisions between flues in old multi flue stacks decay and crumble leading to various often bizarre malfunctions. Soot, sand and masonry appear in fire hearths. Smoke turns up in unexpected places. Even when new they are often badly designed or constructed leading to poor fire heat output, smoking, or rapid decay.

Pretty gloomy but what is worse is the difficulty in finding a builder competent in chimney work. Too often chimney problems are tackled by persons lacking the knowledge to diagnose them correctly and effect a durable remedy. The hapless householder is often confronted with the expense and upheaval of alterations to the fireplace or chimney to find that the problem persists or is worse than before.

What a chimney does

A properly functioning chimney sucks air into the fireplace and this effect is called draft. The suction scavenges air from around the fire into the chimney and prevents stray wisps of smoke from getting into the room. Chimneys that draw in this way are said to have a "natural draft flue", the flue being the space inside a chimney. A chimney draws because it contains a mixture of gases which are hotter, and so less dense, than the surrounding atmosphere. The pressure difference between the top and bottom would be lower inside the chimney than outside if the gases within the flue were stationary. Although this difference is slight, it is what drives gases up the chimney. Interference with draft function cause a fire to smoke.

Design

The recommended flue diameter or size depends the size and design of the fireplace and the height of the chimney. For a two story chimney above a conventional fire the flue cross sectional area should be 1/8 of the area of the fire opening. This is increased to 1/6 if there are other constraints which limit the chimneys draft, the commonest being one story below the roof rather than two. Chimneys should be at least 4m high. Rumford fireplaces have a smaller fire in relation to the size of the opening than conventional designs and flue size can be correspondingly smaller. For Rumford fires up to 1.2 m wide the flue cross section area should be 1/8 to 1/12 of the fireplace open area. For larger fires the ratio can be reduced to 1/10 to 1/15 or less.

In the UK flues suitable for solid fuel burning are termed "class 1". The regulations require that such flues must have a minimum diameter of 175mm, have no sections at more than 45 degrees to the vertical and be lined with approved methods.

Where to locate a chimney is rarely a design choice as it will be dictated by architectural constraints in most cases. Internal chimneys allow improved heating of the building because all sides radiate heat internally and allow back to back fires in adjacent rooms. Chimneys on outside walls on the other hand allow access to soot doors and even ash pits without going through the room. Regulations about chimney design are complex and summarised in the appendix.

Materials

The structure of a chimney can be built from masonry, steel or prefabricated units. Standard brick and type iii mortar are suitable for the most part but for tall free standing chimneys or those with a substantial height above the roof the stronger type ii or i mortar should be used (see chapter 8 for mortar types). Steel reinforcement is needed in areas prone to earthquakes.

Lining

In the UK the law changed in the 1960s to prescribe the ways in which new chimneys are to be lined. Prior to that they were "parged" - lined with a directly applied layer of a lime / sand / dung / horsehair mix. Now chimneys built from brick, blocks, or stone have to be lined either with liners made for the purpose or with a mixture of fired clay aggregate and high aluminate cement. The advantages of lining are insulation to keep the smoke as hot as possible and improve draft, and resistance to chemical attack. A number of systems are on the market. The conventional lining is with fired terracotta "clear" liners. These are made in 230mm and 190mm internal diameters. They have to be rebated at one end and socketed at the other to comply with building regulations and they have to be installed the right way up. The socket must face up. This is so that any water within the chimney will flow back into the flue and not seep out into the surrounding masonry. Clear liners usually present the cheapest material costs of lining systems, though labour savings available from more sophisticated proprietary products may outweigh this.

Type iii masonry mortar is suitable for most brick work and can be used to join flue liners. Type iv mortar is more durable for joining flue liners though it may not be economic to use different mortars for the bricks and liners (see chapter 8).

Pots

Almost all masonry chimneys used for burning solid fuel have some form of chimney pot. The principal purpose of the pot is to prevent or at least to delay chimney decay. Mortars using Portland cement and lime are subject to attack by mineral acids formed by the combination of carbon dioxide and sulphur oxides with water. The smoke from burning solid fuel, particularly from coal, contains various oxides of sulphur which form such acids when they come into contact with liquid water. Low down in the chimney where the temperature is high, little decay occurs by this means. At the top where it is cooler liquid water is frequently present. It originates from condensation of water vapour in the smoke and from atmospheric precipitation. Conditions are ideal for chemical attack of mortars and rapid decay would result if the chimney top were formed from bricks and mortar. The solution to this problem is to use a chimney pot made from a material which is resistant to such attack such as fired clay. The pot should be tall enough that the area where smoke and water mixing occurs is well away from any mortar. It should be at least 300mm long though need not protrude this much above the chimney stack as smoke and water mixing occurs on the inside rather than the outside. Quite commonly the top flue liner is placed to protrude above the stack and act as a pot.

As well as this essential protective role, the chimney pot has other advantages. It raises the effective height of the chimney by an amount that can be quite considerable. Some pots are available that will raise the height 1500mm. This high raise is achieved with a relatively small cost in terms of wind loading because the relatively slender pot catches less wind per m height than does a brick chimney stack. Panel 12 in the appendix shows that the requirement for a chimney not to project more than 4½ times its smallest plan dimension above the roofline applies to the top of the stack not the top of the pot. A pot allows the flue to be heightened while still complying with this rule.

Another significant advantage of using a chimney pot is that a wide variety anti-down-draft types are available. One popular design, the "H" pot, is shown in figure 7.1 and there are many others. In general these designs perform better than clip on anti downdraft attachments. They offer less resistance to smoke egress and are more durable.

Figure 7.1 "H" type anti downdraft chimney pot. This design gives very good protection from downdrafts and little resistance to smoke outflow.

Chimney pots inspire considerable interest, artistry, and creativity and are avidly collected by some!

They are widely available from builder's merchants as plain functional components but there is also a specialist trade in antiques, period reproductions, artistically sculpted shapes, and richly decorated designs. It is almost worth building a chimney simply to serve as a display plinth for one of these creations!

Building a chimney

Building a chimney is quite a challenge because the eye is naturally drawn to it when viewing a house. It is a slender free standing structure where lines that are off plumb are obvious, as is irregular mortar thickness. The level of brick laying skill called for is quite within the reach of the DIY builder but does take some practice. If you do not yet have this skill then it is worth buying some cheap bricks and making up some lime mortar (see chapter 8) and practicing laying the bricks until you are confident with them. Lime mortar is used to make it easier to dismantle practice structures afterwards. When building the chimney take particular care to plumb the corners and keep the structure to the plumb line.

A chimney should be built on a concrete foundation footing as described in chapter 3. The first course of brick is laid around a liner without mortar to obtain the correct spacing. A 10 to 20mm air gap is left between the liners and brickwork to allow for expansion of the liners or for back filling. Building begins according to the dimensions derived from the dry layout with special care to ensure that the first course is square as errors at this stage are liable to be propagated up the chimney. The liners must be the correct way up! The socket end of the liner is up (see detail in figure 7.2). The corners should be plumbed regularly.

The exact design of the bottom of the chimney varies with application. If both a chimney and open fireplace are under construction it will normally be easiest to place the lowest liner above the fire throat. In a stove chimney, access to the flue for cleaning is not usually possible through the appliance so the chimney is extended downwards and a side flue built to connect it (figure 7.2). A soot door is built into the bottom of the chimney, below the side flue, and provision made for a vessel to collect rain and condensation. It is easiest to extend the liners below the level where the stove pipe enters

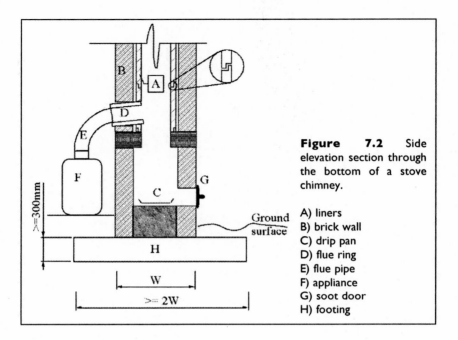

Figure 7.2 Side elevation section through the bottom of a stove chimney.

A) liners
B) brick wall
C) drip pan
D) flue ring
E) flue pipe
F) appliance
G) soot door
H) footing

the chimney. A hole has then to be cut into a liner to admit a "flue ring" or "thimble". This can be done by filling a liner with packed down sand to prevent it from cracking and tapping out the hole with a fine chisel and club hammer or a pointed hammer such as a tile hammer. Chip out small pieces. If large pieces are broken off it increases the risk of the liner cracking. Flue rings should not be exactly horizontal or inclined down towards the chimney. They should be inclined up towards the chimney with a rise of at least 20mm per m so any water runs into the appliance.

The flue ring should have about 80% of the cross section area of the liners. In practice the next size down of liner can be used.

The soot door is placed below the level of the flue ring in a pit into which soot can fall without entering the appliance or blocking the chimney. It should be at least 300mm above the ground if on the outside as the combination of moisture and soot is corrosive to metals as well as mortar. Soot door and frame assemblies are commercially available. They are installed by wiring to the surrounding masonry through eyes provided in the fame before filling around with mortar. The most durable types tend to be made of cast iron.

Common sense indicates that the bottom of the liners should rest on masonry rather than anything corrodible such as nails or steel rods, or flammable such as wood! A header with a hole the same size and shape as the flue can be used as shown in figure 7.2. Resting the liners directly on the footing and cutting a hole in a liner to accommodate the soot door is a possibility but is not recommended because the vessel which must be placed at the bottom of the chimney should be wider than the inside diameter of the liners so that water running down the liner lands in the vessel and not on the footing.

When the chimney is being built for an open fire, access to the flue for sweeping can be gained through the throat. If the flue must pass through a wall the liners can be taken out the side of the chimney and secured in a wedge of concrete as shown in figure 7.3. This avoids the problem of water pooling in the bottom of the flue system but the adhesion between the concrete wedge and the curved liner cannot be relied upon to remain sound after many years of heat cycling. If it loosens the weight of the liners will tend to push the bottom liner down and out of the chimney. This will not happen if the bottom liner rests on a flat horizontal surface and the flue is introduced above this level

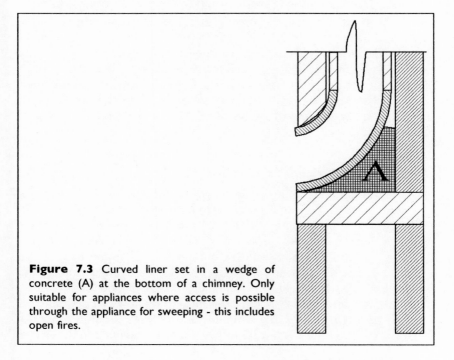

Figure 7.3 Curved liner set in a wedge of concrete (A) at the bottom of a chimney. Only suitable for appliances where access is possible through the appliance for sweeping - this includes open fires.

using a flue ring system as in a stove chimney. Consequently a stove type chimney is a better choice even for an open fire if a simple straight up flue is not practical for other reasons. It also gives the option of installing a stove later.

The rest of the building work is fairly straight forward. Avoid sections inclined more than 30° to vertical if possible and certainly more than 45° to the vertical. Where it is necessary to mortar the liners to the brick work, such as on inclined sections, only mortar one side of the liner so expansion or back filling can be accommodated on the other side. Expansion joints between an ordinary chimney and surrounding masonry are not normally necessary unless it contains multiple flues.

Back filling

The temperature changes in chimneys are smaller in extent and slower than in fireplaces so the temperature differentials found between the liners and surrounding masonry are correspondingly lower. Relatively little thermal expansion has to be accommodated. An air gap can be left between the liners and surrounding masonry but this leaves the stack of liners as a somewhat freestanding structure liable to distortion. It is better to back fill between the chimney wall and liners using a kind of concrete which is a good insulator and is sufficiently flexible to allow for some expansion. A number of proprietary back filling concrete products are available and some recipes recommended in the British building regulations are reproduced in chapter 8. Rapid and large temperature swings as caused by chimney fires *are* liable to crack liners!

Adding a chimney to an existing outside wall

The foundation footing presents special problems when adding a chimney to an existing wall. Footings of both walls and chimneys have to spread the load of the supported masonry over an area of ground. Just how large this area is depends on the local geology. When a chimney is built into a new wall the footing size will be specified by the architect who will take the local geology into account. An architect may not be available when a chimney is being added and so the builder must determine the footing size. As differential settling between new and old masonry is a real risk in this situation the footings should err on the large side. If the house is fairly modern then the excavation necessary to place the footing will expose the footing of the wall. If this is the usual twice the width of the wall then use a footing twice as wide and twice as deep as the chimney. If the wall footing is wider expand the chimney footing accordingly. Steel reinforcement in the footing is not usually necessary but should be considered if the chimney is larger than single flue, taller than 2 stories or the softness of the ground means that it has to be particularly wide. If reenforcement is to be used place the rods 200mm apart 100mm from the bottom of the footing.

The chimney must be securely attached to the wall it is being built next to. The traditional method of doing this was to knock out bricks on alternate courses in the existing wall to allow every other course of the chimney to be let into the wall. This method has the disadvantage that if the chimney settles then cracks may appear between the chimney and wall making the chimney unsafe. For this reason it is recommended that ties are used instead. Various designs are available. They involve raking or drilling the mortar of the existing wall. When choosing remember that they have to withstand heat cycling to modest temperatures. Through bolts are fine but expansion bolts are not recommended for this reason. The mortar joint between the chimney and the wall is liable to cracking so it is recommended that this mortar be raked back 10mm or so and the gap later caulked. If cracks do appear later they are then easy to repair by re-caulking. In general the chimney will only have to be built on three sides but this depends on the wall being at least 100mm thick (see Appendix panel 1)

Figure 7.4 An example of a prefabricated flue block. These are designed to be stacked up forming a complete chimney with integral liner. Some models have holes through the corners parallel with the flue to accommodate steel reinforcement and allow a tall freestanding chimney to be built.

If the flue must pass through the existing wall this can be as a flue liner or ring or as a metal flue pipe (a metal pipe that connects an appliance with a chimney). Traditionally the hole was made by knocking out a few bricks and filling around the flue with mortar but now the job is more neatly done with a masonry hole saw and electric drill. See appendix panel 1 for regulations about the proximity of combustibles to the flue.

Prefabricated flue blocks

Several companies make chimney blocks as shown in figure 7.4. These are made from cast concrete, usually pumice concrete, and include an integral liner. Construction is considerably simplified using these components which are placed one on top of another to the required height. Some include holes in the corners to accommodate steel reinforcement rods to allow tall free standing chimneys to be built. Special blocks with side ports are used for connection to the appliance. As well as being simple to assemble these systems have the additional advantage of being made from good insulators so the resulting chimney will run hotter and perform better than a conventional chimney of the same size. One disadvantage is that material costs will be higher than for conventional construction though this may be more than off set by lower labor costs. Another drawback is that if the chimney is to be constructed on the outside of a building additional masonry is likely to be required as the grey concrete will probably not blend aesthetically with the building. Also additional weather protection may be required.

Above the roof

Flashing is lead, copper or aluminium composite sheeting which prevents water getting between the roof tiles and the chimney. It is let 10mm into the chimney mortar between brick courses and is staggered up the roof slope so that mortar weakening by flashing is spread out over several courses. The chimney stack should extend not less than 600mm above the roof line and not more than 4½ times the shortest horizontal dimension (see appendix panel 12) unless supported. The top flue liner should project at least 150mm above the last course of bricks to act as a pot unless a true pot is used. Some pots have a flange designed go on top of the brick work and this determines how much they extend down into the chimney. If there is no flange the pot is regarded as an extension of the liners and brick is built up to the first course which is higher than the junction of the pot and liners. If an exceptionally tall pot is being used the brick work is extended two courses above the junction. Flaunching is then applied. This is a cambered mortar fillet in the angle between the pot and stack top angled at 30° to 45° to the horizontal. Type iii mortar is not durable enough for chimney flaunching. Type i mortar should be used (chapter 8).

Multiple flues

Chimneys with multiple flues follow similar design constraints to those with one flue. The footing is still at least 300mm thick but reinforcement should be considered. Some solid masonry must separate the flue liners. In the UK this must be at least 100mm thick excluding the thickness of the liners. This corresponds to one wythe of brick. Multiple flue chimneys were widely used before the central heating era but are rarely built in domestic houses now.

Chimney Maintenance

Sweeping

Soot builds up in chimneys that serve solid fuel appliances and DFE gas fires. Eventually this soot build up becomes large enough to cause poor draft because of chimney obstruction, soot falls, or chimney fires. Chimney fires are liable to cause liners to crack because of the swift temperature changes. A soot fall happens when soot builds up to the point where the adhesion between the soot and liner cannot hold the weight of soot deposited. Soot thus falls down the chimney taking lower deposits with it. The result is a disaster, the more so as the room affected is often the best one. The soot falls down the chimney and lands in the grate unless it is a stove type chimney. It blasts into the room on impact and everything is covered - quite disgusting! Sweep chimneys to avoid these problems. Once a year is usual but more frequent sweeping is recommended if the fuel used produces a lot of smoke such as peat.

Pointing

Old chimney stacks need to be pointed every so often. Many chimneys made before the 1960s were lined with a mortar mixture applied directly to the inside of the brick work. Chimneys of this type and more recent ones with leaking linings rot from the inside out. Any defects apparent on the outside probably go right through to the flue. Ultimately the stack will become unsafe if it is not pointed. Pointing must be done so that the mortar goes deep into the joint. A pointing gun is invaluable for this purpose as it is difficult to get deep joint filling with a trowel. If using a pointing gun care must be taken to ensure that cement is not injected right into the flue where it can fall and block the throat or jam the damper!

A bad case is best dealt with by relining the chimney with a system that involves pouring liquid concrete into the space between the chimney wall and flue as the concrete flows into the gaps in the mortar and acts as a full thickness pointing. Poured concrete is used in the rubber hose lining method or as back filling around precast liners.

Chimney problems - diagnosis and cures

Below are described the chimney faults that most commonly cause open fires to smoke. They are listed individually for convenience but in most cases of a smoking fire the cause is either single and obvious, such as a bird's nest blocking the chimney, or less obvious and multifactorial. In the latter case focusing on a single cause can lead to unnecessary expense. This is detailed further in the later section on an economic approach to curing a smoking fire.

The causes of smoking can be divided into design faults and acquired defects. Serious faults in the design of the fire and chimney result in a fire which has always smoked. More commonly a poorly designed or constructed chimney performs OK most of the time but is unduly susceptible to acquired problems. A fire smoking because of acquired defects will once have worked properly. This distinction may help to diagnose the cause of smoking but should not be over stretched. Most commonly when a fire starts to smoke there are several contributing factors. Design may be suboptimal but adequate until there is additional soot build, leaks or adverse winds.

Inspection and testing

The first step of a chimney inspection is to sweep and smoke test it. Sweeping and smoke testing are inexpensive and the smoke test may reveal that relining is necessary. It may be worth knowing this before committing larger sums to a faulty chimney because relining is costly and alone may make the project uneconomic. A smoke test involves placing a smoke bomb in the hearth, lighting it and covering the opening of the fire. The smoke bomb produces large amounts of non toxic cool smoke so that no draft is induced in the chimney. This is important because if the chimney is drawing then air flows inward not outwards through leaks low down and they would not be detected with a smoke test. While the smoke bomb is burning the outside of the chimney is examined for smoke coming out of gaps. This usually means climbing into attic spaces with a torch as leaks are commonest at the top and will be missed unless specifically looked for. Leaks can be difficult to see especially outside if there is a breeze to dispel the smoke. Every inch of the stack should be carefully examined from the ground with binoculars before the chimney is passed. Any smoke escaping may indicate that the stack is unsafe and liable to fall in a high wind.

Camera inspection.

This test is increasingly used by specialist companies. A robotically controlled video camera and lamp are lowered down the chimney. Detailed inspection of the inside is possible. Decay that has not yet led to frank leaks may become apparent. The technique is particularly good at finding partial blockages or collapsed withers (the divisions between flues in multi flue chimneys) as these are usually not apparent on smoke testing. Some systems even allow repairs to be carried out by robotic pointing guns and the like.

Design & construction faults

1) The fire is too big for the chimney

For a conventional chimney over 4m tall the simple rule of thumb is that the diameter of the flue should be constant above the throat and its cross section area 1/8 that of the fires opening into the room. The standard 230mm terracotta liners can thus flue a fire up to 550 × 550mm. The smaller 190mm liners can flue up to 500 × 500mm. For most Romford fires the ratio is 1/10 to 1/15 though the actual flue size is usually larger because of their large opening size.

The rule of thumb and regulations regarding the ratio are in fact quite generous and are designed to ensure that fireplaces are tolerant of poor construction and acquired defects. As fixing a ratio problem is either complex (widening the chimney) or undesirable (lowering the lintel) it is suggested that other ways in which chimney function may be improved are considered before altering it even if the ratio appears to be too small. Only if such an approach fails to cure the problem is an attack on the ratio justifiable.

It is rarely practical to increase the size of the flue to solve this problem. The simpler alternative is to reduce the size of the fire to match the flue size. The easiest way of doing this is to add a hood or drop the lintel though this will lower the thermal efficiency of the fire. Rebuilding the fireplace to a smaller size would be the best solution but is a major undertaking and it would be sensible to try a simpler solution first to ensure that it will work. A piece of board can be cut to cover the top few inches of the fireplace opening and then moved up and down while the fire is burning to see what effect it has on smoking. If this is done over several days it should be possible to find the largest opening size that does not smoke prior to doing a permanent job. The permanent job can be lowering the lintel or raising the grate up on firebricks to reduce the size of the opening.

2) Flue gather is poorly designed

The ideal gather should converge on the throat at about 30° - 45° to the vertical and the inner sides of the gather should be reasonably smooth. Large deviations from this ideal can contribute to smoking either by causing a lot of turbulence in the rising air stream or allowing occasional wisps of smoke to escape or by diverting smoke from one particular area out of the fire out into the room. It is often the outer front corner of fires which smoke in this way. One common problem is a wide horizontal surface under the lintel. Smoke hitting this tends to spread over the surface, most going up the chimney but some coming into the room. It is better to have a design where the flue gather rises towards the throat at not more than 45° to the vertical and forms a continuous curve under the lintel to give a cross section like that of figure 2.4 rather than figure 2.5.

Testing with a smoke taper will show the turbulence and usually identify the causative masonry. The problem may be soluble with a hammer and chisel but will more commonly require fairly major rebuilding to sort out.

3) Air starvation

This problem is more likely in modern or modernised houses than in old drafty ones where the gaps around windows and doors and between floor boards usually provide enough room ventilation. The diagnosis is easy to make as the smoking stops as soon as a door or window is opened to the outside world. Air starvation is dangerous as it can lead to lethal carbon monoxide (CO) poisoning if smokeless fuel or gas are being burnt. The problem is easily solved by installing vents in the room (see chapter 2).

4) Poor chimney positioning

The chimney may be positioned so that the top is in a high pressure area or is prone to collect downdrafts. Both situations arise when tall surrounding structures direct winds up or down. The smoking depends on prevailing wind conditions.

If the chimney is in a high pressure area created by surrounding structures ducting wind towards it then the smoking will be fairly continuous while the wind persists. Atmospheric pressure measurements around the chimney may show the high pressure area to be quite localised and raising the chimney a few feet or moving it some other way may cure the problem but this is an expensive job with uncertain results and a trial with a simple metal pipe placed over the pot to effectively raise the chimney is recommended before permanent changes are made. Another tack is to connect the room to the same high pressure area as the chimney. If opening a window on the windward side of the room solves the problem a vent could be the answer. More elaborate ventilation systems are of course possible but this can be a difficult problem to solve and remember that a chimney fan will almost always work and is not that expensive to install.

If the fire gives occasional puffs of smoke during the adverse wind conditions then it is probably caused by transient turbulent gusts down the chimney. This problem can be solved with a special anti down draft pot such as shown in figure 7.1.

An alternative to replacing the pot is to fit a clip on metal anti down draft cowl top (figure 7.5). These are less expensive that anti down draft pots to buy and fit but are not as effective at curing smoking. The cost of fitting either may be dominated by the cost of gaining safe access to the chimney top in which case a pot may as well be fitted.

Figure 7.5 Chimney with a metal anti down draft clip on cowl top fitted.

Both the problems of high pressure around the chimney pot and downdrafts are at their worst when the chimney is cold because draft is then at its most marginal. Many otherwise perfectly good chimneys smoke on windy days while the fire is starting but then stop smoking once the fire is well alight. The solution to this problem is to use low smoke fuel while the fire is getting going or to light the fire with lots of dry kindling so that a brisk fire gets going quickly.

It may seem from the above that smoking because of downdrafts is an easy problem to diagnose but it is not. A fire which smokes from any cause is liable to appear to be suffering from downdrafts because they are to some extent present in all chimneys in all but the calmest wind conditions. Whether they cause smoking depends on whether the column of rising hot gases in the chimney has sufficient momentum not to be reversed by prevailing gusts. In pre-Rumford fireplaces without throats this momentum was very small and consequently such fires smoked. Similarly anything degrading the speed and laminar flow of the rising column can cause smoking. This is why too wide a throat makes a fire smoke. A briskly burning fire with a gather, no smoke shelf, a throat and a smooth, straight or gently bending flue will produce a column of fast moving laminar flowing gases which is very difficult for gusts to disrupt. Any alteration which brings a fire closer to this ideal is likely to reduce sensitivity to downdrafts. Modern designs which minimise tramp air flow and extract heat from the rising smoke in order to improve thermal efficiency do so at the expense of the momentum of this hot gas column. It becomes cooler and slower moving.

5) Chimney too wide

Sometimes a fire is found which smokes because the chimney is too large. This may occur with the additional and compounding fault of a throat which is too large. The usual situation is of an old building with a large room which was originally entirely dependent on the fire to heat it. Since the building was put up central heating was installed and possibly the room divided. The fireplace has then been reopened and a smaller grate installed than was previously there. The old chimney was perhaps 18 inches by 2 feet in section and has not been relined though a new throat and gather may have been installed. The fire smokes because the chimney never gets hot and the smoke rises slowly and turbulently through it with little momentum and resistance to reversal by downdrafts. Rising gases quickly cool limiting the up-current. If the throat is too large this problem is compounded by excessive amounts of cool room air entering the chimney. The solution is either to reline the chimney or to install a larger fire.

6) Chimney is too resistive for available draft

A problem that can arise with a very tall chimney is that the smoke cools a considerable way from the top. The resistance to air flow up a chimney is proportional to its length and this effect is usually more than cancelled because the draft pressure is also proportional to length and the total resistance is dominated by the throat resistance. The draft pressure only rises in proportion to increasing length if the flue gases remain hot. If they cool the draft pressure rises less than the resistance so with very long chimneys the length can cause a significant resistance which is not balanced by draft. This is a difficult problem to solve and various strategies may be tried. It is rarely possible to shorten the chimney as the height will usually be dictated by the height of the building or environmental factors. Widening the chimney is similarly rarely feasible and liable to failure by compounding the cooling of the smoke. Relining with pumice liners may help but is expensive and it is difficult to know beforehand if it will be successful. One possibility is always to have a vigorous fire to keep the smoke hot. Another is to narrow the throat restricting the amount of cool room air mixing with the smoke and thus raising its temperature though this may itself aggravate smokiness. A chimney fan will solve the problem.

A similar problem can arise if the chimney has several sharp bends or sections that are not vertical. Thirty degrees to vertical is the maximum recommended slope but up to 45° is allowed. The bends and angles increase the length and resistance of the chimney while the draft is calculated only on vertical height so does not improve, in fact it decreases because of the increased cooling effect of a convoluted flue. Again this is a difficult problem to solve as the obstructions which required the bends in the first place are probably still preset. In many cases the obstruction round which the flue us diverted is another flue or fireplace for another room. If that flue is disused then it may be a fairly simple matter to connect the bending flue to the disused one and solve the problem.

7) Siphoning

The term "siphoning" describes the situation where smoke that has been discharged into the atmosphere from a chimney pot is drawn down another chimney and appears in the building but not in the same room as the fireplace. It occurs because the draw of a chimney requires that the room where a fire is burning is generously ventilated. Some of this ventilation can come into the room through other parts of the building. One particular source is down the flue of a second fireplace in another room where there is no fire burning. This kind of reverse flow is usually harmless but becomes a problem if smoke or other fumes are drawn down the second flue as is prone to happen when the top of chimney pots are located very close together. It is the reason why in multiple flue chimneys the pots are sometimes staggered at different heights.

The diagnosis is usually fairly obvious because the smokiest room is not the one where the fire is burning. It can be more difficult in buildings that contain multiple dwellings where siphoning may occur between dwellings. Residents may notice the appearance of smoke without knowing that a fire is in use elsewhere in the building. Nowadays an extractor fan is usually responsible for the draw down the unused flue rather than a fireplace in another part of the building. Smoke may be entering the affected dwelling via a vent which is communicating with a disused flue rather than via an open fireplace. In modern urban environments subject to smoke control legislation the most common annoyance caused by siphoning is drawing in fumes from nearby commercial kitchens rather than of smoke.

A siphoning problem is usually fairly easy to fix. If the second flue (down which the smoke is siphoning) is disused it can be blocked with a chimney balloon* or screwed up newspaper. If the second fireplace is still in use fitting a damper into its throat that can be completely closed when no fire is burning will solve the problem. Alternatively, additional ventilation could be provided in the room with the first fire so that less of its ventilation is drawn down the second flue. Another solution would be to fit a taller chimney pot to the first flue so that its smoke is discharged above the level of the pot of the second flue. This last is the most logical fix but the cost of gaining safe access to the chimney stack is likely to make it the most expensive.

8) Generally poor building

For several decades during the central heating era towards the end of the 20th century, domestic fireplaces and chimneys were rarely built and not all builders retained the required knowledge and skill to construct them properly. They are increasing in popularity again but remain a fairly exacting building task. One occasionally comes across chimneys dating from central heating era that are very badly built. There may be no attempt to fashion a gather with liners plonked straight on top of a fire box. They may be upside down and not mortared. The resulting leaks and throat/gather problems require major surgery to sort out. Total rebuilding is usually necessary by opening up the breast. Relining may be possible but the existing liners will not usually allow enough space to do this and still end up with a class 1 flue. Systems are available to ream out old liners prior to relining but this is an expensive and complicated job. A spray on coating lining system may be an option (see below).

Decay faults

1) Blockages

Chimney blockage by soot, mortar and masonry debris, weeds or birds nests is an obvious and common cause of smoking. A fire that

---

* A chimney balloon is a tough rubber balloon on the end of a hose. It is passed through a fire throat and inflated to block the flue.

smokes dreadfully when lit for the first time after the summer is likely to have this problem. The solution is sweeping. A coring ball may be required. This is a solid iron ball with a diameter 25mm less than the flue that is lowered down the chimney hopefully clearing all before it. Material cleared from the flue this way is liable to stick in the throat. If a coring ball is used take care to examine the throat with a torch and clear any obstructions with a hook or poker.

2) Leaks

Leaks in chimneys cause different symptoms depending on where they are. The pressure in an operating chimney is at or near atmospheric at the top and can be slightly over atmospheric if the pot has a narrow or complicated outlet. Leaks near the top lead to smoke blowing out of the chimney. This matters little if the leak is above the roof line except that it denotes severe mortar decay and the strong possibility that the stack is unsafe and liable to fall! If it is below the roof line the loft and upper story will be smoky. Leaks at the top of a chimney are much the most common because the combination of condensation or rain water and smoke are what eats away the mortar and this mix is found at the top.

At the bottom of the chimney the pressure is below atmospheric – the origin of draft – and so any leaks will draw air into the chimney and will not cause smoke to blow out. If such air inflow is severe it can significantly reduce draft by raising the pressure and cooling the gases in the chimney. This may cause the fire to smoke but the leak has to be pretty big, and above the throat such as would arise from a missing brick or two. Mortar decay alone is not likely to be enough to cause this. The fire in figure 4.3 was an exceptional case where the leak was below the throat. A long disused back boiler had rusted away leaving a huge 300 by 300mm hole in the fireback into a space that freely communicated with the outside. In effect the fire had become a multiple face fire. The diagnosis was not difficult to make and a few firebricks solved the problem!

3) Obstruction by a cowl

Sometimes smoking is caused by a pot top accessory obstructing smoke egress. Various designs of cowl top are prone to this problem. One common cause is a pot cover designed to keep water out of a disused chimney being left in place when the fireplace is reopened. This can be a catch as these pot covers are usually made of the same type of red terracotta clay as chimney pots and may appear to be part of the pot rather than an added accessory. A clogged spark catcher as fitted to chimneys in thatched houses is another common cause of this kind of obstruction.

4) Collapsed withers

Withers are the divisions between flues in multi flue chimneys. Modern building regulations require that there be at least 100mm of solid masonry between flue liners, let alone flues, but in the past these divisions have often been built in a rather insubstantial manner. One method commonly used was to divide up the inside of chimney stacks into flues with slates. Divisions of this kind readily collapse with decay. This leads to holes communicating between flues so that smoke can pass freely from one to another and also the fallen withers may block or partially block the flue below.

Collapse of withers leaves quite large holes between flues and significant leaks can occur. If they are at the top of a chimney they have little effect on the fire's performance but it may be noticed that smoke is coming out of two pots rather than one. Withers defects near the bottom of the flue will cause cool air to be drawn briskly into the flue which will dilute the hot rising gases and reduce draft.

Most of the flues in most multiple flue chimneys are now disused. Decay within a disused flue goes unnoticed and over the years numerous blockages, withers defects and leaks accumulate. A withers defect can arise between a working flue and a complex "system" of blocked, communicating, and leaking flues leading to bizarre malfunctions where smoke may appear out of fireplaces or wall vents that have no obvious connection with the fire in use. Add in a bit of siphoning within the "system" and you can have a major headache. An entire building can become uniformly smoky with no obvious source!

Problems arising from decaying withers are among the most difficult and expensive to remedy. Robotic camera inspection is invaluable in the evaluation of this problem not only for diagnosis but because when withers start to fail it is a sign that the entire chimney withers may be fragile and liable to rapid crumbling. In this situation it can be difficult to reline the chimney with a system that uses back filling liquid concrete like the rubber hose method or liners lowered down from the top because the concrete is likely to flow out of the withers into adjacent flues. These problems can be dealt with using a variety of tricks to support the withers such as placing an additional inflatable rubber hose down adjacent flues and inflating it. The option of tearing down the front of the breast on all floors above the fire and rebuilding the chimney with liners is always possible but disruptive!

An economic approach to diagnosing and curing a smoking fire.

From the above the main cause of smoking may be apparent but frequently it is not. It is then sensible to try solutions starting with those that are simple and inexpensive and moving to those that are more difficult.

A good starting point is to have the chimney swept and smoke tested for leaks. High up they have little effect on draft and smoking but if it should turn out that the chimney has to be relined for reasons of safety or smoke leakage then this relining is likely to at least help if not solve the smoking problem.

Once the chimney has been swept and tested the fire can be tried again. If the smoking problem persists the next thing to do is a careful trial of room ventilation. The fire is burned for long enough to know if it is smoking with a window open. This should be done carefully. Air starvation is potentially dangerous because of the risk of carbon monoxide poisoning so it must be confidently excluded or fixed.

Failing that the next thing depends to some extent on how easy it is to gain safe access to the chimney pot. If access is easy with a ladder then a clip on anti downdraft attachment as shown in figure 7.5 would be a reasonable thing to try first. These consist of a set of baffles that prevent wind from any direction blowing down the flue.

If scaffolding is required then the cost of access will be considerable and to make the most of this cost an extensive survey and repair of the stack and flue is recommended. This should include a robotic camera inspection. The inspection will show any withers problems or blockages. If it is clear then the next thing to try and the most likely to be successful of those so far suggested is to fit an anti downdraft chimney pot if none is present already. There are many designs; one popular type is shown in figure 7.1. At the time of writing they cost around 3 times as much as a clip on attachment but are more durable and better at preventing smoking because they cause less obstruction to smoke outflow.

The next thing to consider though not necessarily do is to lower the lintel as described above. This is easy and virtually always effective if it is lowered enough but is liable to do unacceptable damage to the aesthetics of the fireplace. If the fireplace is of a design where such a change can be tolerated then it is a reasonable solution. As this is a matter of personal taste the owner must decide and not allow themselves to be dissuaded by "experts" whose expertise does not in general extend to aesthetics.

If the problem has not yet been solved then the remaining options save one involve expensive and potentially disruptive building works with no guarantee of success. That one is to fit a chimney fan and this is the point at which I would be inclined to do it. If the chimney is unblocked and free from gross leaks it will work unless the room ventilation is extremely poor which is easily soluble anyway. They consume around 150W of electric power.

Relining old chimneys

The UK building regulations introduced in 1965 specified that all new chimneys had to be lined. Prior to that date most chimneys were not lined in the modern sense. The inside of the chimney was "parged" or coated with a lime mortar. This mortar decays with time and chimney relining is quite an industry with several firms specialising. Most relining is done through the top and bottom of the chimney without having to tear down the breast. Four systems are used to do this. Flexible stainless liners, poured cast concrete, prefabricated liners and spray on coatings.

Flexible stainless steel

This is usually the cheapest method of relining an old chimney. The liner is quite expensive and cost savings are in labour. They are made from double skinned corrugated stainless steel and are slid down the chimney from the top, attached at the top and a hole in the breast is made above the appliance to seal in the lower end above the throat. The drawback is that stainless steel is susceptible to corrosion by sulphur oxides in water and this limits the life of such liners. Guarantees typically extend to 10 years. Stainless steel liners can be used for class 1 flues only if they are being relined and not if being newly built.

At the time of writing flexible polymer liners have just appeared on the market. They are still expensive and there is little experience of their durability but they look promising, being better insulated and potentially longer lasting than stainless steel but with similar labour costs.

Rubber Hose and Concrete

More durable that stainless steel is cast in situ concrete. This system employs a rubber hose which is passed down the chimney and is positioned in the centre with the help of bracing rods and access holes cut into the breast at points of inflection. The hose is filled with compressed air which expands it to the desired flue diameter and liquid concrete is poured around it. When the concrete has hardened the hose is deflated and removed leaving a smooth cylindrical lining. The system is effective and involves only modest masonry works. It introduces a large amount of water into the breast, some of which will soak through and may carry soluble soot products with it that stain the wall days or weeks later. Another problem is that the adhesion between the old chimney and concrete cannot be relied on to maintain the integrity of the liner and so a minimum thickness of concrete must be maintained if it is not to break away with repeated hot/cold cycling. Maintaining this minimum thickness during the process takes care. Needless to say cowboys are available! Unlike some other lining systems, specialized machinery is needed. For this reason cast in situ concrete liners are installed by specialist chimney companies.

Cast concrete liners

The most expensive relining job but the best performing and most durable is to lower specially made concrete liners into the chimney and pour liquid concrete into the gap around them - a process known as "back filling". Such liners are made from pumice concrete. Pumice is an igneous rock most of which comes from Iceland. It is refractory, resistant to chemical attack and contains numerous gas bubbles making it light and a good insulator.

The cost of the liners is comparable with that of a stainless steel liner but considerably more labour is involved. The lowest liner is supported on a plate with two ropes attached in the middle. The ropes are passed through the centre of the liner which is lowered into the flue. When the top 100mm or so protrudes above the stack another liner is threaded over the ropes one at a time, one being used to support the weight of the first liner while the other is being threaded. The second liner is mortared to the first, usually with a wide metal band that is tightened around the joint. This is repeated for all the liners. The installation is easy if you can drop them down a straight chimney with no hold ups but this is rarely the case. More typically the breast will have to be opened in several places to work the liners past inflections and obstructions and this is what makes the system expensive. Once done however the chimney will have the advantages of good draft for its size because the insulating properties of the liners keeps the gases hot, and a long life.

Spray on coating

Proprietary systems are available where a durable lime and cement rendering material is sprayed onto the inside of a flue by a specialised robotic nozzle that is lowered down the chimney from the top. This lining system is not as durable as concrete but has the advantage that the flue is only slightly narrowed. It may be an economic way of rescuing a bad building job because the coating can be applied inside standard liners without reducing the diameter below that required for a class 1 flue. As with the concrete and hose system the job is done by chimney specialists because of the machinery and skills required. Isokern Isokat® is a well established product of this type.

Chapter 8
Materials

Most of the construction of fireplace and chimney installations is done with standard building materials and these are discussed briefly below. The main focus of this chapter is on the more speicalised refractory materials that are used for the parts of the installation that are exposed to the highest temperatures. In general these are expensive and consequently they are used sparingly.

The temperatures reached by components of fireplaces can be estimated from the colour of their glow. Table 8.1 gives the relationship between colour and approximate temperature. The lowest visible red glow which can be seen by the human eye in an otherwise dark environment is given off when an object reaches a temperature of 475°C . Most building materials can withstand temperatures up to about 500°C as long as the temperature changes are not too rapid. If something does not get even slightly red hot it does not need to be built from refractory materials.

Refractory Materials

Refractory materials are those that can withstand high temperatures. Within the field of refractory materials the demands of

Table 8.1. Colour and temperature (°C) of hot bodies	
Lowest visible red	475
Dull red	475-650
Dull to cherry red	650 - 810
Cherry red to orange	810-900
Orange to yellow	900-1300
Yellow to white	>1300
Ordinary electric lamp filament	2500 approximately
Tungsten Halogen lamp filament	2900 approximately

domestic fireplaces are quite modest. The temperatures encountered are relatively low except in the fire box itself and no components are required to withstand both high temperatures and significant structural stress. The biggest demands placed on the resilience of materials in fireplaces is not the temperature itself so much is repeated heat cycling to which they are exposed. Chemical attack by the products of combustion is certainly an issue but is a separate one from refractory resilience as it tends to occur in the presence of condensed water and thus not where the temperature is high. Table 8.2 gives the melting points of a number of refractory materials. Most materials listed are expensive special purpose refractories used for extremely high temperature environments. The ones used in fireplaces are kaolinite, mullite, soapstone and ferrous metals.

Many industrial processes require high-temperature furnaces that must be regularly maintained. There is consequently a large market in refractory materials which are readily available in a wide range of forms. They are a lot more expensive than regular building materials. The cheapest type of firebricks cost about 10 times as much as ordinary red bricks.

Table 8.2. Melting temperatures of some refractory materials		
Material	*Chemical formula*	*Melting point in °C.*
Harnium carbide	HfC	3890
Tantalum carbide	TaC	3870
Carbon	C	3500
Tungsten	W	3410
Lime	CaO	2570
Silicon carbide	SiC	2300
Aluminium oxide	Al_2O_3	2050
Mullite	$3Al_2O_3 \cdot 2SiO_2$	1840
Kaolinite	$Al_2O_3 \cdot 2SiO_2 \cdot 2H_2O$	1728
Soapstone	$3Mg \cdot 4SiO_2 \cdot H_2O$	1640
Iron (pure)	Fe	1535

Even when fire cements are used, the joints between firebricks are the weakest part of a refractory structure so the gaps between them are kept as narrow as possible. For this reason the somewhat haphazard shape irregularities encountered in red bricks are not seen in firebricks which are accurately formed to be flat, square, and true so that they fit together with minimum need for filler. This need for accuracy means that firebricks cannot be cut with a hammer and cold chisel but must be machine cut or purchased in the correct shapes to fit together.

Firebricks come in two common sizes: 9×4½×3 inches (228.6×114.3×76.2mm) and 9×4½×2½ inches (228.6×114.3×63.5mm). They are available in a wide range of shapes some of which are illustrated in figure 8.1.

Fired clay masonry products

Fired red clay is strong, cheap to produce, attractive to look at and remarkably resistant to chemical and physical attack. It is used to make such products as red brick, clear flue liners and terracotta chimney pots. The red colour comes from iron which is a particularly common impurity. For domestic heating applications the melting point of fired clay components is not of great relevance as although variable it is over 1200°C which is considerably higher than the maximum temperature regularly encountered in domestic fires of about 1000°C. Two things limit the temperature range over which fired clay products can be used. These are their resistance to heat cycling and a tendency to crack if heated over 573°C. Fired clay has a coefficient of thermal expansion of about 0.01% per °C, a high Young's modulus* and a low thermal conductivity meaning that if one side of a brick is quickly heated to a high temperature or cooled from a high temperature there will be a considerable temperature gradient across the brick with subsequent differential expansion and internal stresses. The other problem with fired clay is that it contains crystalline silicate (i.e. quartz) particles as impurities. These undergo an allotropic† phase shift at 573°C that alters their volume and shape. The result is that rapid temperature changes

---

* Young's modulus determines how much force is associated with a specific amount of stretch of a material.

† Certain chemicals can take more than one crystalline form or "allotrope". An example is carbon which has allotropes graphite and diamond (and also the newly discovered nanotube). Silicate (SiO_2) is another example.

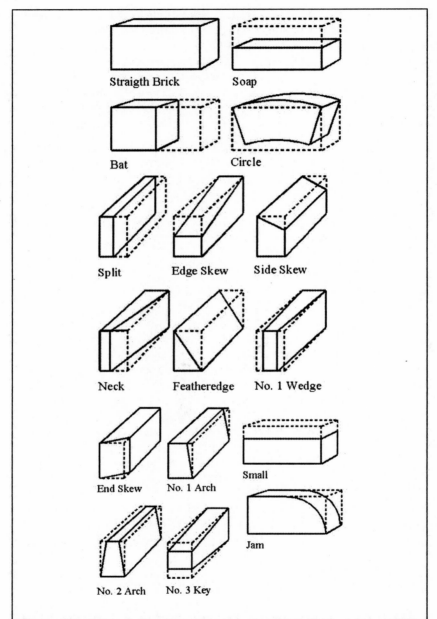

Figure 8.1 Some of the wide range of preformed firebrick shapes available allowing tightly fitting complex shapes to be constructed without having to cut

below 573°C and any excursion of temperature above 573°C readily leads to red brick cracking.

Firebrick

Firebrick is a fairly non-specific term that covers any type of refractory brick. The main constituent of standard firebricks is kaolin as is the case for red brick but iron and other impurities including silicate are removed to increase the melting temperature and reduce the tendency to cracking. Consequently firebricks are light in colour. Kaolinite is cheap but less heat-stable than the more expensive mullite and is often blended with mullite in varying proportions to produce bricks of different grades. Firebricks are graded as low duty, intermediate duty, high duty or super duty with maximum operating temperatures as shown in table 8.3. Even low duty bricks are perfectly adequate for the temperatures encountered in domestic fireplaces and for this reason any firebricks are suitable. This is important to note if there is an inexpensive source of reclaimed firebricks of unknown grade to hand.

As well as coming in different temperature gradings, firebricks also come in two different types: insulating and dense. Only dense firebricks are suitable for fireplace construction. Insulating firebricks are similar to the RCF artificial coal lumps used in living flame gas fires. They are light in weight so have a low volumetric heat capacity and are very poor heat conductors. They are used to line furnaces and kilns because it takes much less energy to heat them up than conventional firebricks. The problem is that they are very fragile. Insulating firebricks can be easily scratched with thumbnail and would not survive the physical abrasion of throwing solid fuel on a fire and

Table 8.3. Maximum operating temperatures of grades of firebrick	
Type of firebrick	*Maximum operating temperature in °C*
Low Duty	1615
Intermediate Duty	1680
High Duty	1700
Super Duty	1745

stoking it for very long. Because of their fragility they do not often appear as reclaim bricks as it is difficult to remove them intact from a furnace lining. The conventional firebricks suitable for fireplace construction are of solid ceramic material, have a stony hard surface that cannot be scratched with wood or a finger nail and are as dense as red bricks.

firebacks are exposed to regular rapid temperature swings and temperatures well over 573°C for which reason they are made from firebricks or other refractory products in preference to red bricks. In the chimney above the fireback and throat, temperature swings are not as rapid or extreme and red brick is used for reasons of cost. The highest point lined by firebrick is usually the narrowest part of the throat or the top of a precast fireback. Even above here dense firebrick will prove more durable and may well be justified if the fireplace is to be heavily used. In the case of masonry heaters where rapid and vigorous fires are burned with direct draft and no cooling tramp air flow, the flue path is lined with firebricks for about 1 m above the firebox.

Refractory Concrete

Refectory concretes, sometimes known as "castable refractories", are water-based and set cold like Portland cement concrete but once set they can withstand high temperatures. The binder is usually Calcium Aluminate cement. Crushed firebrick is the common aggregate. Like firebricks they come in a range of temperature grades that increase considerably in cost with increasing grade and in dense and insulating types. As with firebricks the lowest temperature grade is suitable for fireplace construction and insulating types are unsuitable. While modern castables are durable, they are not quite as durable as dense firebricks. For standard fireplace designs the complexities of mold making and pouring are not justified but castable materials offer enormous scope for the creation of unusual firebacks.

Fire Cement

Ordinary Portland cement is even less heat-stable than red brick and firebricks are assembled with fire cements. These are mortars based on clay and come in 2 varieties: heat setting and air setting. Heat setting fire cement behaves like Potter's clay in that it dries in air but only "sets" when fired to a high temperature. Most fire cement used in the construction of fireplaces is of this type and it works perfectly well. Not much of it gets fired hard because only the lower part of fireback reaches high enough temperatures by this does not present a problem. Fire cement is not called upon to resist great mechanical stresses and what is important is that when exposed to high temperatures it sets hard rather than burns out of the joint.

Air setting fire cement consists of clay and sodium silicate. Despite the different name it works in a very similar way to heat setting fire cement in that it "dries" in air but only sets fully hard when it is heated to high temperatures. The difference is that it dries to a harder more resilient state than heat setting cement. Like heat setting cement it remains water-soluble before it is fired but that generally poses little problem as firebacks don't often get wet.

Soapstone

Soapstone is a soft stone formed from steatite ($3Mg \cdot 4SiO_2 \cdot H_2O$ - also called talc) of igneous or metamorphic origin. It occurs naturally but has so many desirable properties that it could have been designed specifically for use in fireplaces! It has a thermal conductivity which is 4 times that of concrete and 6 times that of brick. It has a 20% higher specific heat capacity than other forms of masonry and is also denser so the volumetric heat capacity is about 30% percent higher. It has a very low coefficient of thermal expansion of 0.0008% per °C. These properties combined to make it extremely tolerant of thermal cycling. Its high conductivity means much smaller temperature differences developed between different parts of the same stone than they do with other forms of masonry and its extremely low coefficient of expansion means that very much less stress arises for specific temperature differences. It is soft enough to be easy to work and hard enough to withstand the abrasion experienced in use and is highly resistant to chemical attack.

Firebacks made out of soapstone are more efficient than those made from other masonry products because the high conductivity means that heat is conducted away from the fireback rapidly so the fireback remains cooler, which gives a high temperature difference between the fire and fireback leading to a faster transfer of heat.

As well as being technically the best material available for building fireplaces soapstone is also rather beautiful with a mottled green or grey appearance that is more attractive than concrete, fireclay, or brick.

Manufacturers use soapstone for a large range of products related to fireplaces and stoves. These include masonry heating systems, smaller stoves and fireplace components such as firebricks, slabs, and formed backs. Soapstone products are more expensive and less readily available, especially in the UK, than fireclay.

Ordinary Portland cement.

Ordinary Portland cement is one of the most useful, ubiquitous, and enigmatic materials used in modern building! It is made by heating a mixture of limestone and silicate such as clay or sand in a kiln to around 1600°C and then grinding up the resulting "clinker" with a small amount of gypsum (hydrated calcium sulphate). Adding water to the resulting grey powder starts a complex and incompletely understood hydration reaction that results in a strong ionic matrix. Exposing this to very high temperatures partly reverses the hydration process resulting in a dramatic weakening of the matrix.

Pure Portland cement sets hard but numerous cracks make it weak. It is much stronger when used in combination with an aggregate such as sand to make mortar, sand and gravel to make concrete, or specialised aggregate for particular purposes. Setting time for Portland cement varies with temperature and conditions but on average it takes at least two weeks to reach its full hardness. As setting is a hydration process the cement must not be allowed to dry out in this period or it will not reach full strength. Similarly it must not be allowed to freeze before setting. The heat from a fire would rapidly dry out any unset mortar in the surrounding masonry so it is important to leave a 2 week period between laying the last mortar joint and lighting a fire in a newly built fireplace. Some recipes for concretes and mortars used in fireplace construction are listed below. All ratios given are by volume.

Back filling insulating concrete

Three options are recommended by the British building regulations for back-filling around flue liners and firebacks:

a) One part ordinary Portland cement to 20 parts suitable lightweight expanded clay aggregate, slightly wetted.
b) One part ordinary Portland cement to 6 parts Vermiculite.

c)   One part ordinary Portland cement to 10 parts Perlite.

Mortar

You make different types of mortar by mixing Portland cement with hydrated lime and sand in varying proportions. The ratio of sand to binder (lime plus cement) is the same as the ratio of grains to intervening space in sand which is fairly constant at 3 : 1 by volume. Five types of mortar are listed below:

Type i (USA type M) mortar has a high compressive strength and is particularly durable. It is recommended for masonry that is below ground and in contact with earth and for tall freestanding chimney stacks and chimney flaunching. The cement : lime : sand ratio is 1 : ¼ : 3¾.

Type ii (USA type S) mortar has a high compressive strength though not a high as type i. It can be used in similar situations to type i but allows somewhat more flexibility. The cement : lime : sand ratio is 1 : ½ : 4½.

Type iii (USA type N) is a good general purpose mortar. It is easily workable and combines reasonable strength with flexibility. It is good for most chimney and rough fireplace opening construction. The cement : lime : sand ratio is 1 : 1 : 6.

Type iv (USA type O) is a weak mortar for internal use where the loads are light. It is flexible and very good at resisting thermal stresses It is good for masonry heaters and joining flue liners. The cement : lime : sand ratio is 1 : 2 : 9.

Lime mortar is weak but easy to tear down. It is the most flexible mortar and was extensively used before Portland cement became widely available. The lime : sand ratio is 1 : 3.

Concrete

General purpose concrete uses a ratio of cement to aggregate of 1 : 5 to 1 : 6. Aggregate may be sold as premixed sand and gravel or the two components may be mixed on site. In the latter case suitable ratios are:

For footings - 1 part Portland cement : 2 parts sand : 4 parts gravel.

For constructional reinforced hearths - 1 part Portland cement : 2 parts sand : 3 parts gravel.

Chapter 9
Combustion

Combustion is the chemical oxidation of fuel molecules. Fuels used in domestic heating are composed mainly of carbon, hydrogen and oxygen. The only products of complete combustion are carbon dioxide and water but combustion is rarely complete. The change from fuel molecules to carbon dioxide (CO_2) and water (H_2O) does not occur in a single chemical reaction but in a series of reactions via numerous intermediate partly oxidised products. In practice combustion is never complete and some fuel and partly oxidised products are left unburned. They act as pollutants and the energy that would be released by their burning is lost. Combustion technology is aimed at minimising the amount of these products that are left. Fuel is burned "cleanly" when this is achieved.

With solid fuels the process is physical as well as chemical. The heat from burning vaporises volatile fuel constituents allowing them to mix with oxygen and burn. It also breaks down large polymers to smaller more volatile products – a process known as cracking. The airborne products of combustion of solid fuels consist of carbon dioxide, water vapour, various partially oxidised products and some un-oxidised molecules given off by vaporisation or cracking.

Wood

Benjamin Franklin, the American scientist and politician who contributed substantially to our understanding of fireplace design, also identified the 3 phases of wood burning. A green log first fizzes as the sap is forced out by boiling water within the wood fibres. Then the wood burns with a bright yellow flame and gives off smoke. The smoke consists mainly of vaporised or atomised hydrocarbon oils and tars with some particulate carbon. The yellow flames are simply burning smoke. The third stage of wood combustion follows when the volatile hydrocarbons have been burned or vaporised and what remains is almost pure carbon as charcoal. This burns with a red glow and faint bluish flames giving off carbon dioxide but no smoke.

These three phases occur simultaneously within a log of any size as the surface will be carbonised to charcoal while volatile hydrocarbons are still being driven off from below the surface and water is boiling away deep within the log. This boiling of water causes the fizzing froth of sap seen on the cut end of burning green wood and also the crackling and spitting of wood as it burns. Pockets of water boil faster than the steam can escape causing the fibres to burst, spitting the overlying charcoal out of the fire. This creates a fire risk and requires a fire guard but adds to the appeal of a wood burning fire. It happens much less with well seasoned wood and stops once all the water has evaporated.

The dry combustible mass of wood is made up of 3 main components: cellulose, hemicellulose and lignin in approximate proportions 45:30:25 by weight. Cellulose and hemicellulose are similar in that they are both polymers of simple sugar molecules, principally glucose. Sugars contain carbon, hydrogen, and oxygen atoms. Lignin is a complex highly branched polymer of monomer molecules that are related to Phenol. The resulting proportions of elements by weight are approximately 6% hydrogen, 52% carbon and 40% oxygen with small amounts of nitrogen and "ash"- mineral constituents that remain after combustion.

The three phases of combustion each involve a loss of fuel mass. The loss associated with the first phase is simply the water content of the wood and varies from around 50% for green soft wood to 35% or so for green hard wood to 10-15% for well seasoned wood. The majority (75-80%) of the dry weight is lost as volatiles in the second phase. The third phase burns the residual charcoal which makes up 18-21% of the dry mass. The remainder is left as ash with soft wood leaving 1-2% dry weight and hard wood 2-4%.

Coal

House coal contains little water so lacks the first phase but otherwise burns in 2 similar phases. The volatile "bituminous" component is driven off as smoke first and burns with bright yellow flames. After this the residual coal is almost pure carbon and burns like charcoal. The difference with wood is that the large majority of fuel mass is carbon which burns in the third phase. The proportion of volatile hydrocarbons that burn is the second phase in correspondingly smaller. The process of making smokeless fuel is similar to the second stage of normal burning leaving a high carbon residue. Not surprisingly, smokeless fuel burns in only one phase: the third phase charcoal type glow.

Air

The main differences between the functioning of different types of heating appliance are connected not so much with their handling of fuel as with their handling of air. The air used by fires and stoves is classified according to how closely it participates in the combustion process.

Stoichiometric air

We can calculate the amount of air needed to bring the exact amount of oxygen fully to burn fuel from knowledge of the chemical make up of the fuel. The amount of air (in kg) required per kg of fuel is known as the stoichiometric ratio. In practice no appliance is perfect and the ratio of air to fuel used is always larger than the stoichiometric ratio.

Excess air

The factor by which air brought into contact with the fuel exceeds the stoichiometric ratio is known as the excess air ratio. The harder it is to ignite and burn a fuel the higher must be the excess air ratio. For example a high performance industrial boiler will typically use a ratio of air to fuel about 5% greater than stoichiometric to burn gas, 10 to 15% greater to burn oil and 20 to 25% greater to burn powdered coal.

A well designed solid fuel stove will require 50 - 100% excess air and an open fire will use 50 - 400% excess air. The amount of heat lost up the chimney increases with increasing excess air.

Bypass air

Bypass air is a term occasionally used to describe air that passes through the fire but does not come into contact with fuel so cannot participate in combustion. This may be significant with fires burning pieces of fuel with large gaps between them but overlaps with excess air and tramp air (see below) in meaning.

Tramp air

Tramp air is air which passes from the room up the chimney but does not pass through the fire at all. It is a feature of open fires. Tramp air flow is necessary to scavenge the smoke from the fire and prevent it from getting into the room. It ranges from 600 to 2000% of stoichiometric air. Tramp air flow is partly responsible for the low efficiency of open fires.

Constituents of Smoke

In an idealised situation all the smoke driven off in the second phase of combustion is burned giving maximum heat yield and leaving no smoke to go up the chimney, the final products of complete combustion being carbon dioxide and water. In practice incomplete mixing of smoke and air and intermittent ignition of mixed smoke and air detracts from this ideal and fires produce smoke containing numerous intermediate products. These are tars, particulate carbon, hydrocarbon oils and carbon monoxide (CO). The more vigorous and hotter the fire and the more abundant the air supply the less smoke is left unburned. It is this effect exploited in masonry heaters that allows them to burn so cleanly despite their relative simplicity.

The smoke production of heating appliances is expressed as the emission factor in g of particulates per kg of fuel used (g/kg). The amount of smoke given off by a bonfire is up to 100g/kg. Open fires do a bit better at around 80g/kg for wood. Masonry heaters achieve 1.4 - 5.7g/kg

Solid fuel burning stoves restrict the air supply to the fire in order to control the burn rate leading to incomplete combustion and smoke. To limit smoke production such stoves include a secondary combustion chamber between the fire box and chimney. This chamber works by mixing the smoke with fresh preheated air. The smoke burns more completely and in so doing keeps the chamber hot (above 500°C). Modern stoves may use a catalyst consisting usually of metal such as Platinum on the surface of ceramic particles to further reduce unburned emissions in the secondary chamber.

Volatile chemicals

Volatile chemicals in smoke range in size. We can isolate them by heating wood in the absence of oxygen and fractionally condensing what comes off. The most volatile molecules are the smallest which when condensed form a clear pleasant smelling liquid known as turpentine. Larger molecules condense into a thicker darker liquid which is also familiar: creosote. The largest volatile molecules form tars. Volatile molecules burning outside the wood give the yellow flames. As larger molecules burn less readily than smaller ones, the smoke that reaches the chimney contains a high proportion of tar and particulate unburned carbon. Such constituents of smoke are pollutants and raise an environmental issue.

Water

Water is the combustion product of hydrogen which is found in all fuels to some extent. Smokeless fuel contains little of it and so gives off little water; wood, gas and oil give off the most.

Carbon Dioxide

Carbon dioxide is ubiquitous as it is given off by all carbon containing fuels, i.e. all practical fuels. It is a product of clean combustion so cleaning the emissions of fuel burning installations of all types does not reduce carbon dioxide output which is purely a function of the amount of fuel used. It forms a weak acid when dissolved in water. It is an important greenhouse gas and its current overproduction world wide is a major cause of concern as there is no easy way of controlling it.

Carbon Monoxide

Carbon monoxide is a particular problem because it is poisonous to man. It has the property of binding to haemoglobin* 200 – 250 times as tightly as oxygen. Inhaled carbon monoxide occupies and hence blocks the oxygen binding sites, stopping blood carrying oxygen, a situation which may be fatal. To make matters worse carbon monoxide

---

* Haemoglobin is the protein in the blood which carries oxygen from the lungs to the tissues. It is red when bound to oxygen and dark blue/black when not. That is why someone who is asphyxiated turns blue. Carbon monoxide binds to haemoglobin in the same place as oxygen, blocks oxygen binding and turns it bright red. This leads to the characteristic flushed bright pink colour of a carbon monoxide poisoning victim.

is colourless and odourless. It is produced when combustion occurs with too little air and poisoning incidents usually arise from poorly maintained and ventilated appliances. Open fires produce some carbon monoxide but their requirement for generous room ventilation and for considerable excess air before solid fuel will burn makes significant build up unlikely. Furthermore, if airborne products of combustion are reaching the room from a coal or wood fire they are liable to make it intolerably smoky long before carbon monoxide levels become dangerous. Smokeless fuel burned in a fire with inadequate room ventilation carries some risk because there is no "smoke warning" if combustion products reach the room. Most carbon monoxide poisoning incidents are caused by poorly maintained gas appliances.

A considerable amount of legislation exists to minimise carbon monoxide poisoning. It is one important reason for the legal requirement that heating appliances are properly maintained. There are various devices on the market which detect carbon monoxide in the atmosphere and they are invaluable aids to safety in areas using gas appliances. As a general rule, if an appliance which is designed to work with a blue flame and no soot is actually producing a yellow flame or soot, then carbon monoxide production is likely and the appliance should not be used pending further investigation. It is not a trivial matter. Approximately 50 people in the UK and 800 in the US die from carbon monoxide poisoning every year and many more are brain damaged.

Oxides of Sulphur

Sulphur dioxide (SO_2) is produce by burning coal or oil. It is a gas which dissolves in water to produces the weakly acidic sulphurous acid. SO_2 reacts with oxygen in the presence of ultraviolet light mainly in the upper atmosphere to produce SO_3 which is a liquid and reacts with water to produce the very strongly acidic sulphuric acid, an important component of acid rain. Wood and peat burning produce insignificant sulphur dioxide.

The combination of sulphur oxides, carbon dioxide and water corrodes cement and metals. Lime added to mortar slows this effect but no amount will overcome it. Such corrosion is at its worst at the top of chimneys where they are coolest and exposed to water condensation from smoke, and to atmospheric precipitation. Chimney top corrosion is so rapid that it is impractical to use a bare brick and mortar stack.

The chimney needs a top which is not susceptible to such chemical attack, i.e. a pot.

Soot

Soot is a black oily powder that is deposited on surfaces exposed to smoke. It is a mixture of particulate carbon and hydrocarbon oils and tars that have been through high temperature flames in the presence of oxygen and yet have not burned. As such soot is composed of large molecules that are difficult to burn so while in principle it is combustible in practice it is fairly inert.

Soot is hazardous to health. High long-term exposure is carcinogenic and was responsible for one of the first occupational diseases to be recognised: skin cancer in chimney sweeps. Soot in the air contributed to chronic bronchitis that was so common in Britain in the 20th century though widespread cigarette smoking was a more important cause. The health risks were the reason for legislative efforts to clean up our air.

Atmospheric soot has been found to be the cause of a serious environmental problem: global dimming. Fine particles in the atmosphere act as foci for condensation of water droplets making them smaller and more numerous than they would be in clean air. This was the cause of the "pea soup fogs" that commonly affected British cities before the clean air acts. The same effect makes clouds more stable and less likely to shed their water as rain. Stable clouds reflect more sunlight back into space so less gets through to the Earth's surface hence global dimming. The major concern is that this recently recognised cooling effect may have masked the true scale of the global warming effect of greenhouse gases. It is technically feasible to clean emissions of soot but not to reduce their carbon dioxide content. Therefore as we clean up our air we may face a double effect of reducing dimming and increasing warming with serious climatic implications within decades let alone centuries.

Chapter 10
Fuel

T he common types of solid fuel used in domestic heating are wood and coal and processed derivatives of them. Also encountered are peat, pine cones, paper and various types of recycled waste. Which fuel is chosen is likely to depend on local availability primarily and only secondarily on consideration of the fuel's technical performance. Appliances are selected to suite available fuels rather than the other way round. Stoves often have quite particular requirements and the availability of suitable fuel must be established before installation. Open fires on the whole can burn any solid fuel the only choice being the size of grate required. The lower the density and heat output of the fuel the larger the grate needed.

Heat yield

Tables 10.1 to 10.3 give the heat yielded by burning various fuels completely. This theoretical maximum heat yield is used to calculate appliance efficiency which is:

$$\text{Efficiency} = \frac{\text{(actual measured heat output into the room)}}{\text{(theoretical heat output).}}$$

This fraction is always less than 1. It is usually expressed as a percentage by multiplying it by 100. A complication is that the theoretical maximum can be expressed as net or gross of water vapour latent heat as explained in chapter 11.

Wood

From a technical point of view wood is not a very good fuel. Its low density and comparatively low heat yield mean more storage space is needed than for equivalent amounts of most other fuels. It is labour intensive to cut, stack, season, and transport from the store to the fire and rots if left without cover for more than a year or two. Even so, where it is available it is the preferred fuel. This is because it is attractive to burn, is a renewable resource and is environmentally friendly. Its smoke is relatively benign having minimal sulphur content and the carbon dioxide produced is balanced by that consumed by the tree during growth. Other advantages are that it is clean to touch so can be handled without tongs and the smoke is often appealing in smell.

Wood has a high, and highly variable, water content. Green wood has around 50% water by weight. It takes about 2.6 Mega Joules (MJ) to heat 1 kg of water to boiling and evaporate it from room temperature so some of the calorific content of green wood is used for this. Moreover the smoke from wet wood is much higher in unburned tars that adhere to the chimney and may cause fires. The chimneys of fires burning wood, especially green coniferous wood, have to be swept more often than those of fires burning coal.

Table 10.1 shows the effect water content can have on calorific value. It refers to net calorific value rather than gross (see chapter 11 for an explanation). One kg of wood with a 50% water content will only contain 500g of dry wood. The maximum calorific value available is in the range 7.2 – 8.7MJ. Of this half of 2.6MJ must be used to heat up and vaporise the 500g of water contained in the wood ending up with 5.9-7.4MJ/kg.

This can be slightly misleading because the same log when dry will weigh less that when wet because of the water loss. Seasoning a log from 50% to 15% water content increases its heat yield net of water latent* heat by around 15%

| Table 10.1. calorific values of various types of biomass ||
Biomass type	Effective Calorific value net of water latent heat (MJ/kg)
Green wood (50% water)	5.9-7.4
Bone dry wood	14 - 19
Peat	14 - 22
Wet peat (85% water)	0-1.1 (theoretical)

---

* The heat needed to vaporise water. Further details are given in chapter 11

The range of calorific values for wood is quite wide. This is partly a consequence of the diversity of types of wood and partly of the range of water contents encountered. The range of volumetric heat yield is even wider because of the additional diversity in the density of woods. In practice volumetric heat yield is a more useful measure as wood stores are built to a specific volume and wood is often sold in volumes rather than weights. Table 10.2 gives approximate values of heat yield per m^3 of stacked wood for various species.

Wood sold for burning in the UK is usually in the form of offcuts, logs or sticks and is sold in sacks containing 15 to 40 kg. In America where wood-burning is more common it is sold in tons or cords were a cord is 128 cu ft (=3.62m^3). This is a stack of 4 by 4 feet by 8 feet long (1220mm × 1220mm × 2440mm). Sometimes wood is sold in "face cords". This is a

Table 10.2. Heat content and characteristics of wood fuels			
Heat yield MJ/m^3 stacked	*Type of Wood*	*Ease of splitting*	*Igniting and Burning characteristics*
High heat 7000-9000	Hickory	Moderate	Ignites easily. Famed for charcoal
	Ash	Moderate	Moderate to ignite. Burns reasonably unseasoned
	Oak	Moderate	Difficult to ignite. Fragrant and makes good charcoal
	Beech	Hard	Difficult to ignite. Burns well unseasoned
Medium 4500 - 7000	Sycamore	Hard	Moderate to ignite. Smoky
	Elm	Very hard	Moderate to ignite. Smoky
	Fir	Easy	Ignites easily. Very smoky with sparks
Low 3800 - 4500	Poplar	Easy	Moderate to ignite. Burns fast with lots of sparks
	Spruce	Easy	Ignites easily. Lots of sparks
	Aspen	Easy	Ignites easily. Lots of sparks and smoky

stack of logs of a particular length that is 4 feet (1220mm) high and 8 (2440mm) feet long but as wide as the length of the logs.

Wood is frequently home-grown and requires cutting and handling. Domestic users generally cut it into logs with a chainsaw and split the logs into smaller pieces with a logging maul or axe. Chainsaws can be highly dangerous, especially the powerful petrol type. Short courses in chainsaw safety and maintenance are available and it is now necessary to have a certificate from such a course before hiring one in the UK. It is not necessary to have proof of competence before purchasing a chainsaw but if you have not been trained it is advisable to attend such a course before using one. There are a number of important technical complications connected with maintenance of safety features on the chainsaw itself, methods of tree felling, and methods of restraining logs for cutting up as well as the choice and use of appropriate safety gear.

Logs over about 150mm in diameter will generally be better split before burning. This can be done with an axe. Better is a logging maul as shown in figure 10.1. This is a narrow heavy axe specifically designed for splitting logs. The one shown has the useful feature of a small prong protruding from the blade. This acts as a hook and allows logs to be positioned before being split without having to put down the maul. A logging maul is designed to be used in conjunction with a sledge hammer. If a swing buries the maul in the log but the log is not split by one blow the maul can be driven in further with the sledge hammer until the log splits.

Figure 10.1 One type of logging maul

Techniques for splitting logs

Small logs are quite easy to split but large ones or ones with knots or branches can be difficult. A log over 450mm or so across can be quite difficult to split down the middle with a single blow from a logging maul. Here are some tricks that can be useful.

If the log has been standing for a while some shrinkage is likely to have occurred and radial cracks may have developed. If they have, striking the log along the cracks is an easy way of splitting it open. Logs generally split most easily in the radial direction but with a large log this would require a complete split. It's often easiest to take small segments off the edges of the log progressively breaking down its size. Take care when doing this because conservation of momentum tends to make the segments fly off horizontally and the axe itself may be deflected in a wide ark as well. Just make sure no one is standing near! Another trick is to wet the sawn surface of the log. The water provides some degree of lubrication between the cleft wood and the sides of the maul blade allowing it pass further into the wood.

Wood Storage

Wood left outside in a damp climate such as that of the British Isles will rot in two or three years. If tree trunks are left uncut they rot more slowly than sawn up wood. As wood rots, its heat yield declines and water content increases making it an ever poorer fuel. The solution is to arrange for wood to be stored under cover. No great degree of sophistication is needed. A lean-too wide enough to overhang the wood stack by 150 to 300mm with open sides is fine. It is sensible to arrange some way for air to circulate underneath the stack to prevent the bottom of the wood becoming wet from water soaking up from the ground. Protected from the rain in this way wood slowly loses moisture content or "seasons". The time it takes for wood to season varies according to the size of the pieces and the weather but after several months the water content of the wood will fall from around 50% to 15 – 20%. This reduced water content makes the wood easy to ignite, less dense and easy to carry, and a more efficient fuel that spits less when burned.

If you intend to burn quantities of wood you will need a shelter for it. With such a shelter you may as well purchase unseasoned wood if available as it is cheaper. It has to be stacked in the shelter anyway so you may as well stack it a few months in advance of use to allow it to season. Buying seasoned fire-wood make sense for occasional users who do not anticipate storing large quantities.

Coal

Coal is ultimately derived from the vegetable matter that formed the jungles of the latest part of the Carboniferous period (360-280 million years ago) in the Paleozoic era of Earth's history. Classical theory holds that extensive areas of vegetation grew over long periods of time and were then buried under rock deposits and ultimately formed coal. This theory has major problems. Coal retains much of the structure of the original vegetation throughout the thickness of seams. Today, vegetation decays and loses its structure far too fast for the lower layers of deep deposits to retain such recognisable structure. Furthermore we find no evidence of a soil layer under most coal seams. They are far too extensive in area and uniform in thickness to be derived from vegetation growing in situ. Yet another problem is that coal occurs in numerous seams with intervening layers of rock. The classical theory requires substantial rainfall to sustain the forests. Over the time needed for the vegetation to grow on the spot this rainfall would cause surface erosion to the rock layers. We find no such erosion.

More credible is a cataclysmic theory. In this the vegetation was deposited by violent hydrological events such as floods or tidal waves. These stripped living vegetation from forested areas and carried it, possibly as log-jams, to areas far from where it grew. These log-jams were deposited in hours or days by the rapid water movements and then just as quickly covered with sediment by subsequent waters carrying slit. In this way whole systems of coal and rock seams could be laid down in a few years or less.

However vegetation found its way into the ground, the pressures and temperatures over subsequent ages resulted in a breakdown of large molecules like cellulose not dissimilar to that produced by combustion. Volatile breakdown products evaporated from the coal seams or "measures" to varying degrees and the vegetation was reduced to a residue made up mainly of carbon. Naturally occurring coal varies in its carbon content from around 60 - 85%. The proportion of volatile constituents remaining in coal varies inversely with carbon content. The higher the carbon content the better quality the coal, the higher its heat yield per kg and the greater its

Table 10.3. Calorific values of various fuels in MJ/kg	
Anthracite	33-34
Good Coal	32-34
Medium Coal	30-32
Poor Coal	22-30
Wood	18
Peat	21
Coke	28.3
Sunbrite	26.8
Coalite	28

cost. As can be seen from table 10.3, the heat yield of coal does not vary very much from one type to another and a more practical consideration is the amount of smoke a coal produces when it is burned in an open fire. Many areas of the western world are subject to legislation controlling the amount of smoke that may be discharged into the atmosphere and burning high smoke fuel in open fires is effectively forbidden in such areas. In accordance with such legislation fuels are classified as "ordinary", "regular" or "bituminous" if they produce too much smoke for smoke control areas or as "smokeless" if not.

Coals with very low levels of volatile constituents are naturally smokeless. Examples are Anthracite and Welsh steam coal (so called because it was used in the past to power steam engines). These coals burn without the familiar bright yellow flickering flames and are more difficult to ignite that dry wood or bituminous coals.

Bituminous coals with higher proportions of volatiles are easier to ignite and produce bright yellow flickering flames and smoke. Such bright yellow flames are one of the most attractive features of open fires and are not produced by any smokeless fuels. Open solid fuel fires in smoke control areas are thus limited in their appeal.

Sizes

Coal is sold in various lump size. The common sizes gradings of singles, doubles, and trebles (figure 10.2) refers to average coal lump

Figure 10.2 Coal lump sizes. Trebles on the left, singles on the right.

sizes of 1, 2, and 3 inches but the actual size range over which each of these names applies varies considerably from one supplier to another. A variety of other terms are used for specific types of coal. For example nuts, beans and grains are often used to refer to anthracite. In the past there were numerous producers all with their own classifications. As an example the Pither company owned their own mine in wales from which they supplied washed anthracite beans specifically for use in Pither stoves. Table 10.4 contains a number of these terms and the approximate sizes to which they refer.

Manufactured Smokeless Fuel

Most smokeless fuel is made from processed bituminous coal or biomass. The manufacturing process involves heating natural coal in the absence of oxygen to drive off volatile constituents and then quenching with water. Manufactured smokeless fuel is less dense than coal so less can be kept in the same volume. It is more difficult to ignite and more expensive.

Gas Coke is a smokeless solid fuel byproduct of the production of coal gas and as such was widely and cheaply available in the past but has all but disappeared from the UK since the country converted to burning Natural Gas.

Table 10. 4. Common terms for coal lump sizes		
Term	*Size mm*	*Uses*
Singles	13 - 35	Open fires, room heaters and some stoves
Doubles	35-75	Open fires, cookers
Trebles	75-100	Open fires
Cobbles	100-150	Large Open fires
Duff	Under 6	Some kinds of gravity fed stove
Beans	15	Gravity fed anthracite burning boilers
Grains	8	Gravity fed anthracite burning boilers
Nuts	25-75	Often refers to anthracite. Open fires and cookers
Large nuts	75-100	Open fires and cookers
Pearls	5	Some boilers

Paper

Gadgets are available which compress old newspapers into bricks for use as fuel on open fires. This is an attractive idea as it disposes of waste and provides a "free" fuel. Such newspaper bricks are not a particularly good fuel however. They have a relatively poor calorific value - lower than wood at about 16 MJ/kg - and are not smokeless. Also they have a considerable ash content mainly due to the kaolin (clay) used in paper making. If only newspaper is used it is not too bad at between 2 and 10 % but rises considerably with other types of paper. The paper used for magazines, books and photocopiers or printers has a kaolin content of up to 30%. Burning it leaves a lot of ash. The time and effort required to make the bricks and dispose of the ash is enough to put off most potential users

Peat

Peat is a vegetable material composed of decomposing grasses and mosses. The plants grow on top of previous generations and after long ages peat cover can build up to many meters in thickness. It is waterlogged in its natural state containing 80 - 90% water by weight. With such high water content the effective net calorific value of wet peat is close to zero and quite possibly negative for which reason it must be dried. When wet it has a similar consistency to heavy cake. In the past it was cut by hand with a special tool into strips measuring approximately 50×100×2000mm. The process is now mechanised. The cut pieces are left undercover to dry or have the water squeezed out of them mechanically. The basic finished "sod" is a dry crumbly brick measuring about 25×50×200mm. In this form it is bulky and difficult to handle and therefore it is only used extensively close to areas where it can be cut. Peat has a fairly high calorific value of 21 MJ/kg. It is not very dense in basic form and thus the calorific value per unit volume is low. Of all solid fuels in common use peat produces the most smoke and requires an increased frequency of chimney sweeping. On the plus side it has a very low sulphur content and is admired for the quality of flame and smoke it produces.

Peat is very common and a small proportion of the total world stock is cut for fuel (and increasingly for horticulture). New peat is being produced faster than it is being removed on a worldwide scale but on a local scale it acts as a nonrenewable resource because it forms so slowly. In many parts of Europe, burning peat stopped simply because they ran out of local supplies. This is true of Germany and the Netherlands. Some geographical features are a consequence of peat cutting. An example is the Norfolk Broads. These are a series of lakes that were created by cutting peat in large quantities to be burned in London. Peat is still widely used as a fuel in many areas particularly Ireland and Russia. The city of St Petersburg gets 17% of its electricity supply from a peat burning power station!

The performance of peat fuels can be improved by processing. Briquettes are made by compressing and drying the peat to produce dense blocks that are easy to handle, store and ignite. Their lower water content gives them a greater heat yield per kg than sod peat and they produce less smoke. Peat based smokeless briquettes are also available.

Oil

Heating oil is rarely used as a fuel for open fireplaces but several designs of stove are available. An advantage of oil over gas is that it burns with a more attractive yellowish flame giving stove designers more aesthetic scope and unlike solid fuel stoves the glass in stove doors are not so prone to blackening with soot.

Oil burning appliances are sometimes used in places where there is modest need for cleanliness and oil is freely available. They range from sophisticated stoves to simpler open fires where oil is dripped onto a pile of RCF coals in an open grate where it burns. These are often installed in vehicle work shops where waste engine oil is used as fuel.

Gas

Most open fires installed today in the UK burn gas, and most gas is Natural Gas. This comprise chiefly methane (CH_4). Natural Gas is found trapped under domed impervious rock layers within the Earth. It origin is not so clear as for coal and oil. The prevailing theory is that it comprises the most volatile elements given off in the creation of oil and coal deposits from organic matter. It has also been suggested that it does not have an organic origin but dates from the formation of the Earth's crust. Wherever it came from it is a clean and convenient fuel.

Other forms of gas are propane and butane and mixtures of them. These are used mainly in remote areas where a mains gas supply is not available. Their principle application is in firing cooking stoves and heating boilers. Living flame type gas fires that burn propane or butane are available but are not often chosen because these gases are more expensive than natural gas and places with no mains gas are generally not in smoke control areas and are likely to have a ready supply of wood, making solid fuel open fires a more attractive option.

Chapter 11

Heat

Basics of heat and energy

Heat is not an easy concept to define so it is fortunate that we have an intuitive idea of what it is. It is that property that an object has more of when it is hot than when it is cold. It is also fortunate that heat behaves in a simple way that is easy to understand and predict.

Heat is a form of energy (another difficult concept to define). Quantities of heat are measured with the same units as quantities of energy. The SI unit (Système International d'unités) of energy is the Joule (J). In terms of domestic heating, 1J is not very much. It takes about 100,000J to heat enough tap water to boiling point to make an ordinary mug of coffee. For this reason the kJ (equal to 1000J), MJ (equal to 1000,000J) and GJ(1000,000,000J) are more commonly used.

Most heating calculations involve the rates at which Joules are given off by a heater or absorbed by its surroundings rather than total numbers of Joules. Such rates are expressed as Joules per unit of time. The SI unit of time is the second (s) and rates of heating are expressed in J/s. The J/s is such a widely used unit that it has its own name: the Watt (W). Rate of energy conversion is called power so the unit of power is the Watt. As with the Joule, the Watt is rather small so we usually quote kW (1000W) or MW (1000,000W) or even GW (1000,000,000W).

A somewhat perverse unit is the kilowatt hour (kWh). Like the Joule this is a unit of energy but it is expressed in terms of power multiplied by time. The unit is used because it is easy to reckon total energy usage of appliances by multiplying their power in kW by the time for which they are in use in hours. 1kWh = 1000W×1 hour =1000W×3600 seconds or 3600,000J (or 3.6MJ)

Temperature is another awkward quantity to define. Object A is hotter than object B if heat flows from A to B. The rate at which this heat flows is proportional to the difference between the "hotness" of A and that of B. The term "temperature" refers to this degree of hotness and is measured in degrees. Fahrenheit (°F), Centigrade (°C) or Kelvin (K – notice that the ° symbol is not used for Kelvin) are in common use. Converting between °C and K is fairly simple as the units are the same size but the scales start at different temperatures. Absolute zero (0 on the Kelvin scale) is -273.15 °C so temperature in K is temperature in °C+273.15. Fahrenheit is more complicated because the units have a different size and the scale starts at a different temperature. Zero °C = 32.00°F and one degree on the centigrade scale is equal to 1.800 or 9/5 degrees on the Fahrenheit scale. Degrees C = (°F-32)×5/9 and °F = (°C×9/5)+32.

Before the SI units were introduced the English speaking world used the BTU (British Thermal Unit). The heating industry has been particularly slow to change and the old BTU is still frequently encountered in the UK and is in general use in the USA. The BTU is a unit of energy like the Joule. It is the energy required to heat 1 pound of water by 1°F. Originally this is how it was defined but now it is defined as 1055.05585262J. Rather confusingly it usually appears not as the BTU of energy but as a unit of power. It would be nice if this unit of power was the BTU per second as it would then be close to 1kW but that, of course, would be too easy. It is BTUs per hour and the unit is usually abbreviated to BTU. What is more the BTU per hour is not much power (=0.293W). Domestic heaters are in the range 5,000 – 150,000 BTU per hour so quite often 1000 BTU per hour is also abbreviated to 1 BTU! It is usually obvious from the context what BTU is meant.

Specific Heat Capacity

The specific heat capacity of a material is the amount of heat energy required to raise the temperature of a unit of mass of that material by one unit of temperature. In SI units this is the energy in J required to raise 1kg by 1K*. The word "specific" in this context means

---

* Strict scientific definitions use degrees Kelvin (K) rather than degrees centigrade (°C). As the size of the units is the same it makes no difference which scale is used when working with differences between temperatures and it is generally convenient to stick to familiar °C for practical purposes.

per unit of mass or weight[†] (the kg in S.I. units). The heat capacity of an object is equal to the specific heat capacity of the material from which it is made multiplied by its mass. The Volumetric heat capacity is the heat capacity per unit of volume rather than mass and is equal to the specific heat capacity times the density of the material. It is more useful than the specific heat capacity when quantities are reckoned in volume rather than weight as is the case for most masonry. Both specific and volumetric heat capacities vary slightly with temperature but not enough materially to affect our calculations as a high degree of accuracy is not required. Some useful heat capacities are listed in table 11.1.

There are various things to note from table 11.1. The first is the very high heat capacity of water, both specific and volumetric. Another is that all types of masonry used in building have similar heat capacities of about 840 J/kgK or 1950 J/lK. For calculations it is usually good enough to assume these values for all masonry. The exception is soapstone, a rock with an unusually high heat capacity and also a high heat conductivity. It is very soft. Two of its main applications are in teaching sculptors to carve and in making fireplaces and stoves.

Latent Heat

Heat energy must be transferred to change the state[‡] of a substance. It takes 420kJ to raise 1kg of water to from 0 to 100°C but to turn it into steam at 100°C requires a further 2.26MJ! This amount of heat is called the specific latent heat of vaporisation of water. It is not of great relevance to fireplaces and heating as even if water is involved in heating radiators etc. it is not boiled away. It is of relevance to fuel combustion because some solid fuels contain water that must be vaporised as they burn and the heat required to do this detracts from

---

† Mass and weight are not actually the same thing. Mass is a measure of the amount of matter in an object and is defined by the rate of acceleration the object experiences when subject to a particular force. Weight on the other hand is the force of gravitational attraction on the object, which is proportional to its mass. Weight therefore varies with local gravity whereas mass does not. On Earth 1kg of Sugar has a mass of 1kg and a weight of 1kg. On the moon 1kg of sugar has a mass of 1kg but a weight of 165g! Strictly all properties referred to here are per unit of mass not weight but on earth they are virtually the same.

‡ "State" means solid, liquid, or gas. Changing state means melting, freezing, boiling , condensing, or subliming (solid to gas). Latent heat must be added to melt or boil something and removed to freeze or condense it.

their heat output. Green wood and peat have the highest water content. Freshly cut peat may contain so much water that it cannot be burned because less heat is available than is required to dry it out! Latent heat is also relevant to a curious oddity about the way the heat output of fuels and hence the efficiencies of heating appliances are calculated in Europe and the USA. Virtually all fuels release water vapour when they burn. This water comes from hydrogen within the fuel which is oxidised to water or trapped water which is vaporised. If this water vapour is

Table 11.1 heat capacities and densities of some materials used in buildings.			
Material	*Specific Heat capacity J/kgK*	*Density kg/l*	*Volumetric heat capacity j/lK*
Dry air at 20°C	1160	0.00120	1.4
Water at 20°C	4180	1	4180
Bricks and mortar	840	2.2 - 2.4	1850-2020
Building stone	840	2.5	2100
Concrete	800	2.4	1920
Glass	820	2.6	2130
Granite	800	2.7	2160
Asbestos	840	1.6	1340
Marble	880	2.6	2290
Soap Stone	980	2.5-2.8	2450-2740
Cast Iron	545	6.8-7.8	3700-4250
Steel	517	7.5-8	3880-4140
Copper	395	8.9	3520
Brass	395	8.4-8.7	3320-3440
Lead	129	11.3	1460
Aluminium and alloys	900	2.5-2.8	2250-2520

condensed to liquid water it gives up 2.26MJ/kg in latent heat. The calorific value of a fuel can be calculated with this latent heat (gross) or without it (net). Common usage in the USA is of gross calorific values whereas in Europe net values are used. For this reason American figures for calorific values are higher than European and efficiencies of appliances are correspondingly lower.

Heat requirements of buildings

Accurate assessment of the power required to heat a room or building adequately depends on a knowledge of the thermal conductivities or "U" values of the walls and ceilings and the expected difference in temperature between the inside and the outside. Such data will be available in the planning and construction stages of new buildings but is not likely to be to hand thereafter, particularly for old buildings. In these cases estimates are required. Most domestic rooms in temperate climates require between o and 6kW to heat them depending on the time of year. A better estimate is that in temperate climates average domestic rooms require up to 100W per m3 of room space.

A more accurate estimate still can be obtained from the formula:

$$\text{heat requirement in kW} = (80A + 300B + 20CD)E$$

where

A = area of wall or ceiling in contact with the outside in m2
B = area of glass in m2
C = number of room air changes per hour
D = volume of room in m3
E = temperature difference between the room and outside in °C.

This formula contains terms for the loss of heat by conduction through the walls, ceiling and windows (80A and 300B) and another term (20CD) which refers to ventilation losses.

A comfortable environment requires ventilation of living spaces by the constant inflow of fresh air and outflow of stale room air. When heating rather than air conditioning are in use the fresh air is cooler than the desired room temperature and must be heated. The heating power required to warm this incoming fresh air is referred to as ventilatory loss and as with other powers is expressed in Watts. Calculating ventilatory loss is fairly straightforward. It is simply air flow in l/s × the temperature difference in °C × the volumetric heat capacity of air at atmospheric pressure: 1.4J/l°C. As in the formula above air flow is often expressed as the number of times the air in the room is replaced each hour or "air changes per hour".

As an example I will calculate the ventilatory heat loss induced by a typical domestic open fire. Suppose in a room of 65m3 (a moderate sized room) there is an open fire with draft flow equivalent to 4 air changes per hour. The outside air temperature is -3°C and the room temperature is 20°C. What is the ventilatory loss?

The amount of air lost up the chimney is 65×4 = 260m3/hour or 72 litres/second

The heat lost per second is therefore 72×(20-(-3))×1.4 J/s

=2318W.

If the outside temperature falls to -20°C, not at all uncommon in northern latitudes in the winter, this figure rises to 4032W. These figures are quite realistic and illustrate one of the main problems of open fires. As a heat output into the room of 2-6 kW is typical it is easy to see how negative efficiency figures can arise. The actual heat loss up the chimney is much higher than this because the rising gases are heated considerably above room temperature. The importance of the ventilatory loss is that the heat lost in this way comes out of that often small fraction of the fires total heat output which usefully heats the room.

Calculations like those above are all very well if we know the rate of ventilatory air flow. Needless to say we usually don't! The requirement for comfort in most rooms most of the time is a ventilation rate of ½ to 2 air changes per hour.

Open fires induce considerably more ventilatory air flow than is required for comfort and this is one major source of their inefficiency. Figures are typically between 2 and 10 air changes per hour. This compounds the problem of calculating the heat requirements of a room for the purpose of selecting an appropriate open fireplace. Even if the current ventilation rate is known it is not known how much extra air flow will be induced by the fire itself.

If it is important to make an accurate estimate of heat requirements in cases where the above calculations are likely to be misleading, for example in odd shaped rooms or particularly exposed buildings, then an experimental approach is possible. This is based on the observation that the heating power required is proportional to the difference between the temperatures of the room and the outside air. The method is to heat the room in question exclusively with heaters whose heat output in Watts is known. It is usually most convenient to use electric heaters for this purpose as they can be assumed to be 100% efficient and their power consumption in W is printed on the appliance. Ensure that all other forms of heating are either of known power output or are turned off. Note the total power required to keep the room comfortable. Add on 140W for each adult in the room§ while the experiment is in progress to get P, the total heating power. Measure the inside and outside temperatures. The outside temperature is T and the comfortable room temperature is R. Then consult meteorological statistics for the area to find the coldest outside temperature at which the room is likely to have to be adequately heated. This temperature is called C. The power required during such conditions can then be calculated as

Maximum heating power required = $P \times (R-C)/(R-T)$

Even this can be in error if for example high winds significantly affect the cooling of the outside of the house or induce cold drafts and it does not take account of the unknown increased ventilatory loss a fire would cause.

Supplying heat to a room

Once the heat requirement of the room has been estimated we can chose the heating appliances. If direct electric heating is to be used then it is a simple matter of adding the power consumption figures on the appliances to get the required amount. This form of heating is unlikely to be economic. The alternatives present greater difficulty in calculating the heat output.

In the case of central heating, radiator outputs can be calculated from the manufacturer's data and the temperature of the water which in turn can be calculated for the boiler manufacturer's data. The term "radiator" is a bit of a misnomer as 80% of a radiator's output is convective and only 20% is radiant. Table 11.2 gives a guide to the heat output per m^2 of radiator area for various types. The total output when filled with water at 75 °C in a room at 20 °C is also given. 55 – 85 °C is

---

§ 140 W is the heat output form an adult not engaged in heavy exercise or sleep.

a typical range for the output temperature of water from a boiler in a domestic central heating system.

Stoves have outputs specified by the manufacturer though these will assume that the appliance is operating at maximum efficiency which is generally only achieved when the output is near its maximum and the stove is in good repair. Stove efficiencies are between 40 and 75% for solid fuel fired, greater for gas or oil fired.

Open fires

The increase in air flow and ventilatory heat loss induced by open fires can be unpredictable. Worse is that the efficiency of fireplaces is so variable that the heat output can be equally difficult to estimate. The effect of ventilatory heat loss can bring the efficiency of an open fire below 0% and 40% is about the limit for the most efficient designs. This means that choosing a fireplace for a room is inevitably more hit and miss than choosing other heating appliances and is one reason why I recommend that if an open fireplace is to be installed provision should be made to adequately heat the room entirely by other means.

Fireplaces may be inefficient but that does not mean that they are not powerful. An open fire with an efficiency of 25% burning ordinary coal at a modest rate of 1kg per hour will provide 2kW of heat to the room and lose 6kW up the chimney. A grate 400mm wide by 225mm deep (a standard size in the UK) can comfortably consume 2.5kg/hour and dissipate 5kW into the room and 15 up the chimney. The problem is not so much that heat production is inadequate but that it is

Table 11.2. Heat output from central heating radiators		
Radiator type	*W/m²°C*	*W/m² with water at 55°C above room temperature*
Plane single panel	22-25	1210-1375
Plane double panel	35-40	1925-2200
Plane triple panel	48-54	2640-2970
Designs with added fins single panel	27 - >150 depending on type	1485->8250

Table 11.3. Approximate heat output and room sizes for coal fires		
Grate width	*Max. power*	*Approximate room size m³*
400	6kW	35-75
450	7.5kW	50-100
500	9.5kW	75-125
550	11.5kW	100 +

expensive in terms of fuel use and unpredictable in that one fireplace with and efficiency of 40% will dissipate 8kW into the room for the same amount of fuel burned as another with 10% efficiency which dissipates only 2kW into the room.

Table 11.3 gives a rough guide to the heat output into a room and approximate room size that can be adequately heated by the 4 commonest sizes of coal fire used in the UK. These are very rough figures. The lower limits placed on room sizes are arbitrary as there is no meaningful lower limit on how small a fire can be burned in any size of grate.

Wood burning fires are different again because the heat output of wood per l is only around a third that of coal. A wood burning fire will need to have a grate about 1.4 times as wide (and so have about twice the area and contain 3 times the volume) for an equivalent heat output to a coal fire. The larger fireplace opening means greater ventilatory heat loss but a damper is more likely to be fitted. The size of wood fire needed adequately to heat a room is less predictable than for coal but broadly a grate width around 1½ times those given for coal in table 11.3 will be about right.

Appendix
Chimney Building Regulations

Building regulations vary somewhat from place to place and time to time but there is a close similarity between the main points that are aimed at safety and fireplace performance. What follows is an overview of the regulations in the UK. The most significant difference between the UK regulations and other areas is that here we do not have to allow for earthquakes. In America there are extensive requirements for chimney reinforcement in earthquake prone areas.

Many of the regulations are simple common sense. For example the foundation of the chimney must be able to bear the dead weight of the entire chimney and any wind loads that will be encountered. It must be build entirely of non combustible material. The chimney must be positioned so as not to risk igniting surrounding combustible material via direct heating or sparks leaving the top. An obvious problem is in thatched houses where the thatch is vulnerable to spark ignition. Extra care is necessary and a spark catcher will help. Chimneys must be accessible for cleaning via the appliance or via a soot door.

Other regulations are more complex than those covering fireplaces and hearths which were covered in chapter 3. In order to ease reading the following requirements for chimneys are arranged into panels containing both diagrams and explanatory text.

Panel 1. Chimney cross sections

For any chimney the flue liner must be surrounded by solid material at least 100mm thick and the same must separate the liners of adjacent flues. In the figure below A, B, C, D and E must be ≥100mm. An additional restriction applies to chimney walls less than 200mm thick. This is that no combustible material may be installed less than 38mm from the wall with the exceptions of picture rails, dado rails, skirting boards, floor boards, mantel pieces and architraves.

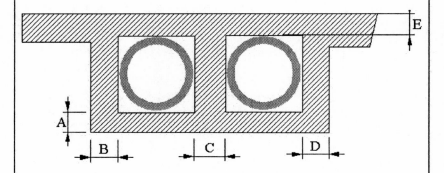

When one side of the chimney forms part of a solid wall between two dwellings then this wall (thickness E) must be at least 200mm thick below the roof:

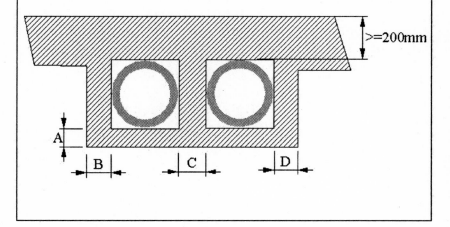

Panel 2. More on chimney cross sections

A slight variation on panel 1 is where the wall between two dwellings is a cavity wall. In this case each wythe must be at least 100mm thick. A, B, C, D, E and F must all be ≥100mm:

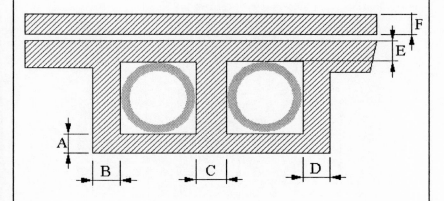

Chimney breast serving 2 dwellings

The requirements for the walls separating dwellings or buildings are again slightly different in cases where flues are back to back in one breast. Here all dimensions must be at least 100mm:

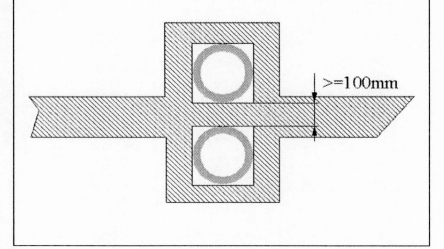

Panel 3. Class I flue dimensions

Class I flues must have a minimum diameter (the internal diameter of the liners, A below) of 175mm. There are several requirements for flue lining but in essence flues must be lined with liners designed for the purpose and fitted together with cement between them and they must be installed the right way up! Flexible metal liners do not conform to class I unless used for relining.

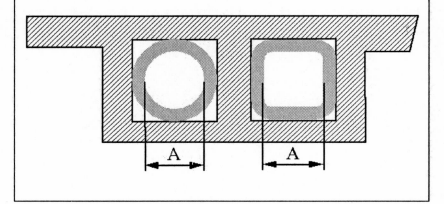

Panel 4. Offsets in flues

Offsets in a flue route it round obstructions, usually other fireplaces and flue systems. The flue must at all points be inclined at not more than 45 degrees to the vertical.

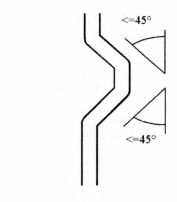

Panel 5. Soot Doors

Flues that terminate in a class I appliance (A) which does not allow adequate access for chimney cleaning must have a soot door (S) at the bottom and must be able to hold a vessel to collect condensation and rain water from the chimney.

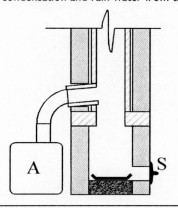

Panel 6. Flue Pipes

Various types of appliance, particularly solid fuel stoves, are connected to the chimney flue by a specially made pipe called a flue pipe. Flue pipes can be made of cast iron or mild steel not less than 4.75mm thick. They can be made of a variety of other materials which satisfy the regulations. In essence flue pipes designed for the purpose can be used in the country where they are commercially available but not necessarily elsewhere. Flue pipes are hot and pass through the living space so not surprisingly they are subject to tight regulation. They may not pass through any walls, ceilings, or floor. The exceptions are that they may pass through the wall of a chimney in order to connect with the flue and they may pass through a ceiling and floor which carry a chimney suspended above the appliance in which case the floor section through which the flue pipe passes must be made of non combustible material or be protected from the heat of the pipe (panel 10).

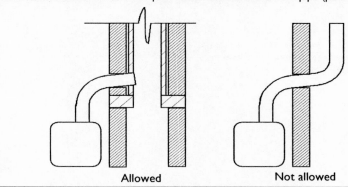

Allowed   Not allowed

Panel 7. Naked flue pipe passing through combustible floor or ceiling

No combustible material is allowed within three diameters of the flue pipe as it passes through a chimney or external wall or ceiling unless special provisions are made.

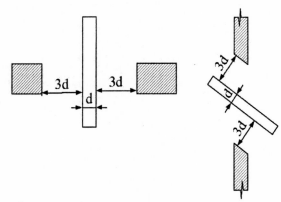

Panel 8. Flue pipes passing through combustible walls or ceilings protected by non combustible material

If a flue pipe passing through a combustible wall or ceiling is surrounded by a non combustible material then the gap between the pipe and combustible material can be reduced to 200mm around and below the pipe and 300mm above it:

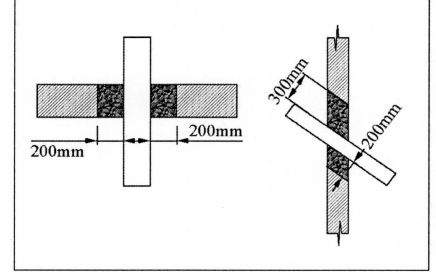

Panel 9. Flue pipes for open fires

Sometimes an open fire appliance that cannot be used as a stove is fitted in a much larger fireplace and a flue pipe is a convenient way of connecting the appliance to the chimney above. In this situation the flue pipe may be of mild steel not less than 1.2mm thick as long as the distance to the chimney is not more than 460mm.

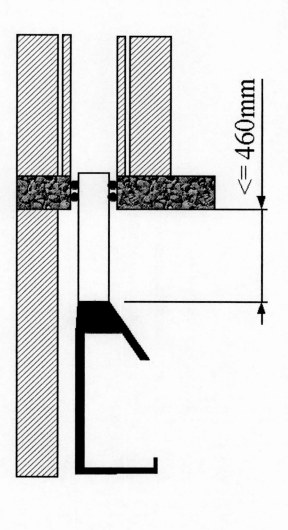

Panel 10. Flue pipe protected by a sleeve designed for the purpose and passing through a hollow combustible roof or wall

Such sleeves are made of asbestos cement (or asbestos free equivalent) or they consist of two concentric cylinders with insulation packed between them. The cement or insulating layer must be at least 25mm thick. There must be a gap of at least 25mm between the sleeve and the combustible material and the combustible material must not be closer to the flue pipe (inside the sleeve) than 1½ times the diameter of the flue pipe. The sleeve must extend at least 150mm beyond the combustible material in either direction.

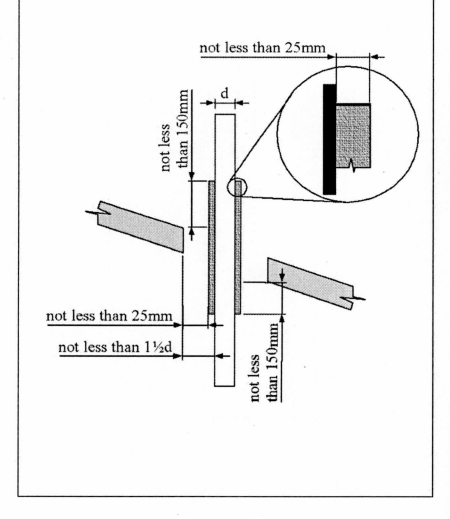

Panel 11. Flue pipe protected by a sleeve designed for the purpose and passing through a solid roof or wall

The requirements are more stringent with solid walls or roofs because they do not cool as well as hollow ones. In this case the flue pipe must be at least 190mm from any combustible material and the gap must be filled with non combustible material not less than 115mm thick.

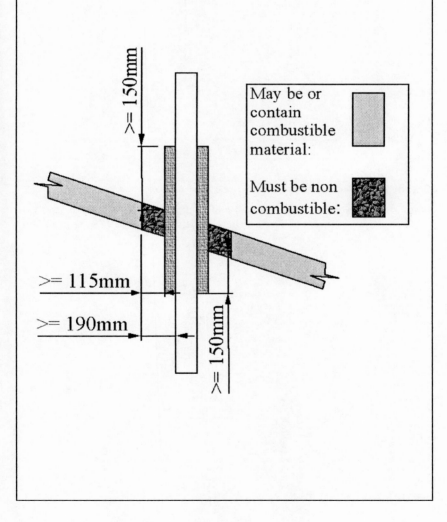

May be or contain combustible material:

Must be non combustible:

Panel 12. Height of chimneys above roofs

A chimney must project at least 1m above the highest point of attachment to the roof and must also project at least 1m above the highest point of any window, ventilator, opening or part of another building within 2.3m of the chimney. The stack should project not more than 4½ times its smallest plan dimension above the highest point of attachment to the roof.

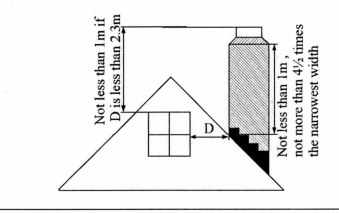

Panel 13. Chimney close to the crest of a steep roof

An additional constraint applies if the roof is pitched at more than 10° and the chimney is within 600mm of the ridge. In this case the chimney must also project at least 600mm above the ridge.

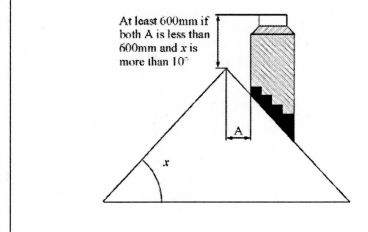

Panel 14 Special rules for prefabricated chimneys

There are several prefabricated types of class I chimney on the market which consist of tubular sections supported by attachment to the surrounding secure structures. An example is chimneys made from two concentric metal cylinders the space between them being filled with a thermal insulator. The rules regarding these types are complex but as they are proprietary products, comprehensive fitting instructions come with them. In general they must be accessible for inspection and maintenance along their entire length. Their outer surface runs hotter than the outer surface of a conventional masonry chimney and some extra care is needed to protect surrounding combustible materials. If such a chimney passes through a storage space such as a cupboard it must be surrounded by a removable casing with a gap between the casing and the chimney. Another consideration is that the joins between sections are the most likely places for leaks to occur and these joins must not be located within a floor, ceiling, roof or wall.

Index

Summary

This book gives a careful and comprehensive explanation of how open fires work. The emphasis is on the technical aspects of their operation. All the information needed to design, construct and operate open fires plus their chimneys is included. The principles of draft and air flow are described. The details of design optimisation to maximise attractiveness and thermal efficiency of fireplaces and throats are explained in detail.

The history of fireplace design is traced from Roman times trough the heyday of open fires in the late 19th and early 20th centuries to their subsequent replacement by other heating systems and recent revival as items of beauty. Included are chapters on the principles of combustion of solid fuel, choice of fuel, principles of heat, materials used in fireplace construction, choices of grate and gas fires.

Essential reading for anyone involved in fireplace design or maintenance be they architects, builders or DIY enthusiasts.

Printed in the United Kingdom
by Lightning Source UK Ltd.
116830UKS00001B/227